How to
Instantly
Connect
with
Anyone

LEIL LOWNDES

Mc
Graw
Hill

New York   Chicago   San Francisco   Lisbon   London   Madrid   Mexico City
Milan   New Delhi   San Juan   Seoul   Singapore   Sydney   Toronto

The *McGraw·Hill* Companies

Library of Congress Cataloging-in-Publication Data

Lowndes, Leil.
    How to instantly connect with anyone : 96 all-new little tricks for big success in
relationships / by Leil Lowndes. — 1st ed.
        p.   cm.
    Includes index.
    ISBN-13: 978-0-07-154585-3 (alk. paper)
    ISBN-10: 0-07-154585-9 (alk. paper)
    1. Social skills.   2. Interpersonal relations.   I. Title.

HM691.L69   2009
646.7′6—dc22   2008045686

5 6 7 8 9 10 11 12 13 14 15 16 17 18 19 20 21 22 WFR/WFR 0

ISBN 978-0-07-154585-3
MHID   0-07-154585-9

McGraw-Hill books are available at special quantity discounts to use as premiums and
sales promotions or for use in corporate training programs. To contact a representative,
please visit the Contact Us pages at www.mhprofessional.com.

This book is printed on acid-free paper.

Contents

 # Introduction

What Determines Social and Professional Success?

For all the hair styling, shoe shining, suit buying, and personality projecting we do, we never really know why some people succeed in life and others don't. Some highly successful and beloved people are shy. Others are boisterous. Some big winners in life are sophisticated. Others are simple. Many introverts are esteemed, while some extroverts are shunned. And, unless you are auditioning to host the Academy Awards, your personality and looks are not the keys to becoming beloved and successful in life. So what is the key? Will this book help you find out?

Let me tell you what this book will do—and what it will not do—and then you decide. I do not guarantee you will soon be chatting comfortably with a commodities broker about crude oil futures. Nor do I assure deep discourse with a doctor of philosophy on his dissertation. What I do pledge, however, is that you will be able to meet people confidently, converse comfortably, and quickly connect with everyone you encounter.

You have probably already discovered the invisible personal and professional glass ceiling constructed solidly over your head, my head, and everybody else's head. This book will help you craft a weapon to smash this invidious enemy by mastering communication subtleties you may have never even known existed. And, of course, it will also tell you how to avoid saying and doing those "dumb little things" that make people disconnect from you—thereby losing their potential business, friendship, or love.

You will also learn how to give them an extraordinary gift, the gift of self-esteem. This is something that, sadly, people seldom consider when dealing with others.

How do you do this?

Let's Go to the Laboratory to Find Out

You and a professor of psychiatry walk into a lab and see two naked men sitting in straight-back chairs, wearing nothing but embarrassed smiles on their faces. The professor mercifully throws each a blanket while explaining your assignment for the day.

"These two gentlemen," he informs you, "both work in a multinational corporation. One is the CEO. He has a loving family, faithful employees, and adoring friends. He has enough money to enjoy life, care for everyone he loves, and even donate generously to charity.

"The other," he continues, "cleans floors at the company. He, too, is a good and honest man. However, this fellow has a string of failed relationships and few friends, and he has trouble making ends meet.

"You, my dear student, are to determine which is which."

You look at the two men quizzically. There doesn't seem to be much difference between them. They look to be about the same age, of comparable weight, similar complexions, and, if it can be determined by looks, equal intelligence. The professor walks toward the men and lifts the bottoms of the blankets, revealing four bare feet. "Is this a hint?" he asks you.

"Uh, no," you respond, bewildered by his insinuation that it might be.

He then pulls the blanket up higher to reveal their knees and thighs. Walking back to you, he asks, "Is this a hint?"

Now you are more befuddled. You shake your head no. As the professor returns to the blankets, you close your eyes and fear the worst. Then, you haltingly open them. You *and* the gentlemen under the blankets breathe a sigh of relief. The professor has merely revealed their heads and upper torsos.

He strokes his goatee, looks at you piercingly, asking the same question with his eyes. You look at one man, then the other, then back at the first. Neither would make the cut for a *Cosmo* centerfold, but you would classify both as handsome.

"I'm sorry, I can't tell who has which job," you respond.

The professor is not surprised. He continues, "What if I were to tell you that both men were born into families of the same socioeconomic status, grew up in the same neighborhood, played together as children, went to the same schools, and tested similarly on an IQ test?"

Now you are completely flummoxed.

If It's Not Looks, Intelligence, Education, Money, or Upbringing, What Is It?

Have you ever been similarly confused? You see two people who, from all outward appearances, are similar. Yet one is successful, the other a failure. One lives above that glass ceiling where only winners dwell. The other looks up longingly, asking himself, "Why are they up there, and I'm still struggling down here?"

Some people think the big boys and big girls residing above the glass ceiling are shielding their turf and won't let anyone else in. That's not true. They *want* you to break through. It can be lonely up there. In a sense, they are auditioning you to be one of them.

I have several actor friends who, after not "making the cut" in an audition, don't realize the directors are even more disappointed. They are desperate to find the right person to cast. Likewise, big winners long to find others to welcome to their club. Like all of us, they want to enjoy the company of companions on their own level. Unfortunately, many people who think the big cats are biased don't recognize that their own blunders barred them from being accepted.

Back to the Laboratory

The professor repeats his question. "Which of these gentlemen is the CEO and which cleans the floors?"

You shrug, "I give up."

The professor smiles, turns to his subjects, and says, "Thank you gentlemen, you may go now." They are as thankful as you that the experiment is over. Grasping their blankets tightly around themselves, they stand.

Subject number one turns to subject number two and says, "Bet you're glad that's over, Joe. Good job!" Walking out the door, he looks at you and says, "I know that must have been an uncomfortable experiment for both of you. I hope the next is pleasanter. You must be doing very important research."

As subject number two starts to leave, he says, "Glad I could help you out." He pauses for a moment at the door, looking expectant. The professor hands him some money. Subject number two quickly takes it and starts to put it in his pocket . . . until he realizes he doesn't have one.

The professor closes the door and once again asks you the big question: "So, my dear student, which is the CEO and which is the cleaner?"

With a big smile, you confidently reply, "The first is the CEO."

"Right!" The professor is ecstatic. "And *how* did you know?"

You conjecture, "Well, the first fellow was concerned with the other man's feelings, and ours too. The other guy, come to think of it, said '*I* am glad *I* could help you out,' putting the emphasis on himself. That made it sound like we owed him something."

"Exactly!" With a eureka expression, the professor clarifies, "You see, the first gentleman put himself in the other person's mind-set, thus creating an instant connection with him. He predicted Joe's discomfort and complimented him to alleviate it.

"The second fellow, because he had the 'you owe me' attitude, encouraged me to 'pay him off.' Thus we have no further debt to him."

You agree, "Yes, whereas if the first man asked us a small favor, even years from now, we would gladly grant it.

"Uh, but Professor," you hesitantly ask, "Why were they naked?"

He answers, "The reason I stripped them of their clothes for this experiment was to shrink their comfort level and thus see how each would react in a strange or new situation—as we all must do daily."

The professor looks at you. "Did you sense how much more confident the CEO was? That was because he predicted how the other fellow felt being put in that painful position. Therefore, his own discomfort took a back seat. Do you remember his first words? 'Bet you're glad that's over, Joe. Good job!' He sensed that Joe needed a self-esteem booster.

"He was also confident because, over the years, people have given him their respect and warmth. And why is that? Because he treats everyone the way he did the three of us. He predicted our various emotions and responded accordingly.

"The CEO also thought about *our* emotions. He understood that conducting an experiment with two naked men was probably uncomfortable for us as well. Do you remember what he said?"

You do. "He forecast our emotions and expressed trust in the significance of our research. He then wished us well."

The Difference Between Winners and Losers in Life

The CEO displayed what I call *Emotional Prediction*, or EP. He was able to predict how Joe, the professor, and you would feel right after the experiment. With just a few sentences, he connected with everyone and made them feel more comfortable.

Some people instinctively possess this heretofore unnamed quality. Unfortunately, the majority doesn't. EP is so complex that people can seldom predict their *own* emotions, let alone those of others.

In a study published in the *Journal of Personality and Social Psychology*, researchers queried students in the weeks before a major exam about how they would feel in the hours immediately before and just after the test. Later, the researchers asked them about their feelings just before grades were posted. Finally, the researchers inquired, "Precisely how will you feel if you pass? What about if you fail?" Very few students could accurately predict what their own emotional reactions would be.

That's where *you* come in. By the time you have finished this book, you will sense other people's emotions, even before *they* understand them. You can then connect with them accordingly. This does not mean you have to be a CEO, or even want to be. It does mean, however, you must have Emotional Prediction to achieve your highest goals—whatever they are in life. Whether it is winning friends, finding love, getting a better job, or just being able to connect with people.

How Does Emotional Prediction Differ from Emotional Intelligence?

Good question. *Emotional intelligence* is the concept Daniel Goleman fleshed out in his excellent book of the same name. It involves (1) knowing your own emotions, (2) managing your own emotions, (3) motivating yourself, (4) recognizing emotions in others, and (5) handling relationships.

Emotional *Prediction* is yet another layer of communicating. It is *predicting ahead of time* what someone's immediate or distant emotions will be in reaction to something said or done. You can then orchestrate your own behavior accordingly, usually to reinforce the confidence and self-respect of those you are dealing with. This, in turn, augments their affection for you and boosts your own self-confidence. Why? Because you will soon be in the habit of reacting sensitively to others and thus receiving positive feedback from everyone.

The majority of people's reactions to you are subconscious. Their quicksilver responses bypass the brain and go right to their "gut." Malcolm Gladwell's well-researched book, *Blink*, proved and popularized the concept. People no longer doubt this unseen reality and the pivotal role it plays.

Emotional Prediction Is Vital for Love to Last

I have often wondered how people who once loved each other, lived together, even created a child or built a company together can wind up in a state of mutual loathing.

More than 40 percent of today's marriages end in divorce, many of them bitter. If partners are blind to each other's emotions, their loving moments can morph into hidden hostility. People often hold their explosive feelings inside like undetonated grenades. Then one day, he says one more thing that confirms, "He's a dictator." Or she does something that absolutely proves, "She's a twit!"

That is the tipping point. When the couple recognizes that they receive more *pain* from the relationship than *pleasure*, one of them pulls the pin. The injuries are intense. The couple splits.

Psychiatrists and psychologists have acknowledged the "pleasure-pain principle" since 300 B.C., when the Greek philosopher Epicurus put pen to papyrus. Sigmund Freud, often credited with creating the concept, fleshed it out in his tomes.

More recently, megamotivator Tony Robbins (of walking barefoot on hot coals fame) danced around the stage shouting about his theory that people run toward that which is pleasurable and race away from that which is not.

Whatever packaging of the concept one prefers, the time-honored truth is this: The pleasure-pain principle affects all our relationships. The tiniest ways you touch someone's life add up. If you inadvertently give someone enough negative feelings, she soon wants you out of her life. On the other hand, if each time she comes in contact with you, she leaves feeling better about herself, she will reward you with respect and affection.

We are not talking about giving compliments here. That's Dale Carnegie stuff from seventy years ago. Nowadays, overt compliments are clunky and obvious. To win people's respect and affection, you must dig deeper into their psyche and locate the site, size, and shape of their fragile self-esteem. Once accomplished, you can accurately predict their emotions, respond with sensitivity, and make them feel connected to you.

Let's Revisit the CEO and the Floor Cleaner

The naked CEO in the laboratory echoed your emotions and those of the professor. When he said, "I know that must have been an uncomfortable experiment for both of you," that wasn't obvious praise. He merely expressed awareness and predicted how you might feel about conducting the strange experiment.

In contrast, the floor scrubber spoke only of himself. He expressed no perception of how you and the professor might feel. You can see how his selfishness and lack of sensitivity could be a tiny pinprick—let's call it a "pain prick." Since it was your only contact with Joe and you had no others to offset it, it was sharp enough to deflate any desire you might have had to do things for him or to see him again. Throughout his life, this poor chap had probably let too many pain pricks pile up with people. No one promoted him from floor scrubber.

Someone's ego is like a hemophiliac with unspeakably thin skin. The slightest prick causes profuse bleeding. If you thoughtlessly give someone enough tiny pricks of pain, their internal bleeding ego tells its landlord, "Stay away from him or her. It's dangerous for me!"

Anchor Yourself to Pleasure, Not Pain

Neurolinguistic programming, or NLP, is a form of psychotherapy developed in the 1970s. The philosophy's advocates would say the floor scrubber had "anchored" himself to pain. In fact, if someone had a few more negative experiences with Joe, just spotting him would invoke unpleasant feelings. I know a woman who, for years afterward, suffered extreme nausea passing the hospital where she had had chemotherapy driving to work. She chose a route that made her commute twenty minutes longer just to avoid it.

The NLP teachings tell us if you, say, tap your nose each time you feel happy, just tapping your nose will re-create those joyful feelings. I haven't tried the happy nose-tapping bit. However, just seeing a photo of certain people and children in my life fills me with joy. In other words, they are anchored to joy.

The following 96 unique communication skills, which we will call "Little Tricks," will help you anchor yourself to pleasure in people's lives. After using several of these techniques with someone, she will feel joyful seeing—or even thinking—about you.

If you have found yourself doing any of them already, smile and applaud yourself. You have Emotional Prediction. This rare quality comes naturally to some people, but most of us have to learn it. I sure did, many times the hard way. Often I will tell you how.

Before we begin, let me tell you about two unusual contributors to this book.

Dogs and Cats

Charlie Brown's dog, Snoopy, was America's most beloved pooch for half a century from 1950 to 2000. Snoopy was a little beagle with big fantasies and a Walter Mitty complex.

He was the master of everything—at least in his daydreams atop his doghouse. Yet he never said a word. His thoughts floated up in cloudlike balloons connected to his head by a series of small bubbles. In the cartoon biz, this is called a "thought bubble."

Just like Snoopy, everyone has unspoken thoughts. They play a big factor in *How to Instantly Connect with Anyone*. Since I don't have a bubble key on my computer, I will put the secret sentiments of the person I am writing about in italics. They wouldn't express their thoughts out loud.

But they are thinking them, just like Snoopy.

Cat lovers, your favorite animal also plays a role in the book. You will come across the name "big cat" a number of times. Why do I call people that? Because we're talking about what many call the human jungle. When two lions, tigers, or cougars encounter each other in the jungle, they slowly circle each other. With steely eyes, they carefully calculate which of them has the stronger survival skills. People in the human jungle do the same—some consciously, some unconsciously. However, they are not staring at size, sharp teeth, or claws. The crucial survival factor is skill in communicating well with other cats in the human jungle.

Since the designations "big shot," "big wheel," "big cheese," and "big enchilada" carry negative connotations, I will call those who have mastered communication skills *and* Emotional Prediction "big cats." Like the naked CEO, big cats are always conscious of themselves, their surroundings, the current situation, and other people. They make a concerted effort to harmonize all four.

Why Is Much of the Book Aimed at Making People Respect *Me*?

Many of the following Little Tricks are techniques to enhance your own confidence and prestige. You might think this is incongruent with the goal of helping others feel good about themselves. It is not, for this reason. As much as people would like everyone to respect them, they long for acceptance from someone they look up to.

The need for this type of appreciation starts early. Preschoolers want approval from their parents. Kids want the admiration of their teachers. And teens crave acceptance by the cool crowd. Even as adults, people still yearn for recognition from those they respect.

When people revere you, your deference in dealing with them gives their self-esteem a powerful boost. And, as you become more sensitive to their sometimes suppressed emotions, their affection and esteem can turn into genuine love for you.

In Defense of Manipulation

Countless kindhearted readers have asked me, "But, Leil, aren't some your Little Tricks manipulative?"

For my answer, let's go back to the Roaring Twenties. Specifically 11:45 P.M. on January 16, 1920. That was the moment when Americans could legally have their last drink in the United States for what turned out to be thirteen years. Prohibition of liquor took effect at midnight.

A wise politician, when asked if he were for or against Prohibition, answered:

> If, by alcohol, you mean the dangerous drink which destroys families, makes husbands monsters, beat their wives, and neglect their children, then I am fully for Prohibition. But if, by alcohol, you mean the noble drink which promotes good fellowship and makes every meal a pleasure, then I am against it.

I'd like to draw a parallel here. If, by manipulation, you mean using circuitous, unfair means to get something out of someone, sway them to your way of thinking, cheat themselves or others, or do something solely for your own benefit, then I am against it.

But if, by manipulation, you mean predicting people's emotions and helping them feel good about themselves, gain confidence—and at the same time enjoy your company and value their relationship with you—then I am for it.

I sincerely hope you'll use the 96 Little Tricks in that spirit. And I pray that everyone you come in contact with will benefit from your having read them. If afterward, they just happen do something nice for you, it was not your manipulation. It is merely a happy by-product.

Ask not what you can do to make them like you.
Ask what you can do to make them like themselves.
And then they'll love you.

PART ONE

Seven Little Tricks

to Make a Great Impression Before People Even Meet You

How to Develop Excellent Eye Contact in Ten Easy Steps

Ever since Mommy yanked you out from hiding behind her skirts and told you to look people in the eyes, you've known how crucial good eye contact is. In the Western world, it signifies honesty, respect, interest, intelligence, candor, and confidence. Yet, for many, the most difficult aspect of meeting people is looking into their eyes long enough to really connect with them. Why is this a challenge, even for some self-assured people? Because, like tigers staring each other down in the jungle, intense eye contact ignites a primitive fight-or-flight instinct. If the tiger looks away, it could get pounced on. Weak eye contact is a handicap in the human jungle, too. Here is a ten-step physical therapy program to strengthen your eye contact.

While gazing at someone, slowly describe the color of her eyes to yourself. Don't stop at blue or brown, light to dark. There are sapphire, pale, and ice blue eyes. Brown eyes can be hazel, almond, or earthy. Grey can range from light slate to dark storm cloud. Sometimes we've known people for years and can't accurately describe their eye color. Think of half a dozen friends. Can you picture the precise color of their eyes?

The second time you look at the same person, check out the shape of her eyes. Are they round? Oval? Almond? How much of the whites of her eyes are showing? And how white are they? A bit bloodshot?

Here is another crutch for the "eye-contact challenged": Study how far apart her eyes are. Ask yourself, "If she loaned me her binoculars, would I have to separate the eyepieces or bring them together?"

Are her eyes symmetrical? Is one eye a little smaller or droopier than the other?

Another time, concentrate on the length of her eyelashes. Are they straight? Curly? What color are they?

When you are with a small group, watch each person's eyes to determine whom he is looking at most.

When extended eye contact is called for, such as when someone is speaking, count his blinks. A study reported in the *Journal of Research in Personality* called "The Effects of Mutual Gaze on Feelings of Romantic Love" proved that people who were directed to count each other's eye blinks during a conversation developed stronger romantic feelings than members of a control group who were given no eye contact directions.

Here are a few more ways to train yourself to become comfortable with maintaining excellent eye contact. Try to determine if he is wearing contact lenses. And are the lenses colored or clear?

If he is wearing glasses, are his eyes in the center of the frame? A bit above? A bit below? Are they bifocals?

This last one is for women only. Determine how much eye makeup another female is wearing. Mascara? Shadow? Eyeliner? (Stop laughing, gentlemen, we women do that naturally.)

If you practice these ten techniques, looking into someone's eyes will gradually become more natural and less daunting, without depending on these crutches.

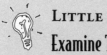 **LITTLE Trick #1**

Examine Ten Characteristics of Their Eyes

To boost your eye contact with people, alternate between defining the color, shape, and whites of their eyes. Check out the length and color of their lashes. Are they wearing contact lenses or glasses? How far apart are their eyes? Count their blinks. Determine whom they are looking at most. Ladies, check out a woman's eye makeup. Is she wearing false eyelashes? Meow.

After a few months of doing these exercises, looking into peoples' eyes will be a breeze. Strong eye contact will be second nature.

After you have practiced Little Trick #1, you graduate to a strategic way to use your eyes—when appropriate.

How to Use Your Eyes to Make People Crave Your Approval

In certain circumstances, the following facial expression can be quite potent and help you achieve your goals be they professional, social, or romantic.

As an example, I'll take the latter because it's a personal story of how Little Trick #2 helped me "take the tumble."

I was on a cruise ship called the *Homeric*. One night, I and a group of other fawning passengers were invited to sit at the captain's table. While someone else was speaking, I happened to see Captain Accornero's face. He was looking at me and—BLAM!—his expression made me want to be a blob of putty in his hands. His head was tilted, his brow was furrowed, and he was looking at me intently with slightly squinted eyes. The expression gave his face an intensity, as though he were searching for something. Giorgio seemed to be assessing me, judging me. It gave him a superior demeanor. I felt like a Roman gladiator praying for the thumbs-up from the emperor.

But, I must admit, I liked it. When Giorgio's lips softened into a smile, it was as though he had saved me from the lions.

Sadly, months later after we started dating, I realized Giorgio was not using the scrutinizing expression as a "capture Leil" technique, although it unquestionably achieved that goal. The reason for his searching look was that, as a ship's captain, he spends many nights on the ship's bridge searching for signs of other vessels through dense fog. That's why I call this Little Trick "Searching Eyes."

First let me tell you how to make the expression, and then I'll share some suggestions on where and why to use it.

How Do You Make Searching Eyes?

Imagine yourself driving on a winding country road in a sparsely populated part of the country. The night is inky black—no moon, no street lights. Suddenly, a dense fog encircles you and your car stalls. You pray there is a house in the distance so you can call for help. You get out of the car, squint your eyes, and search intently through the thick fog for any sign of light.

You have now have executed Step One of Searching Eyes.

Step Two: Finally you see the distant headlights of a car coming your way. At last, help. Your face relaxes and a slight smile softens your lips.

The first phase of the expression gives people the impression that you are evaluating them—not in an unfriendly way, but thoughtfully. Then, when they see the second phase, they will interpret your expression as contemplative acceptance. Therefore, they value it all the more.

How to Use It in Business

Searching Eyes is an effective tool in the corporate world. It demonstrates contemplation behind your final approval of an individual or even of an idea someone has just presented. It puts you in the superior position of evaluating them. Hold the expression for as long or as short as the situation demands.

Women, because people sometimes view us as too accommodating, this Little Trick is an especially powerful professional tool for us. It combats that weaker image and makes you appear more authoritative. Resolve to use it in certain situations, most particularly when dealing with old-style sexist male managers.

How to Use It Socially

When you are meeting potential friends, definitely tone down the first phase of the expression to just a flicker. However, showing a brief second of Searching Eyes before your warm "hello" makes you look more heartfelt and genuine. After that, be sure to keep good eye-friendly contact when communicating with that person.

How to Use It for Romance

Gentlemen, Searching Eyes unquestionably has an interesting effect on women—as you've seen from my experience with the captain. When used appropriately, it can to make her anxious to win your approval.

Conversely, women, if you plan to use Searching Eyes on a potential romantic partner, tread gently. Most men fear rejection and will interpret it as such. Make Step One exceedingly brief before granting him your smile of acceptance.

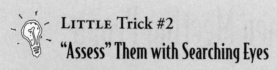

LITTLE Trick #2
"Assess" Them with Searching Eyes

Whenever you deem it appropriate—whether you are judging an idea, a business proposal, or a person—momentarily give a slight scrutinizing expression. Then, if and when you are ready to seal the deal or win their warmth, morph it into a slight smile of acceptance. They now feel they have "won" your approval.

Of course, to make them feel that your approval is, indeed, a prize they've won, you must come across as a confident individual, someone who is confident in his or her own skin.

Here's how to prepare for that—before you even meet them!

How to Wear Confidence When Meeting People

The next two Little Tricks should be regular practice for ladies, gentlemen, and their offspring who want to feel confident at important meetings, parties, or the first day of kindergarten.

One summer, a sizable law firm invited me to give a seminar called "The Corporate Image." The audience consisted mainly of paralegals, administrative assistants, and a smattering of attorneys. Their company culture was conservative, and, of course, I had to set a good fashion example. However, I had the constant female complaint, "I don't have a thing to wear." I needed a summer suit to express a cool corporate image—a splendid excuse to go on a rare shopping spree.

After not finding a suit at a dozen reasonable shops, I wandered into an overpriced boutique, with no intention of actually purchasing anything there. But there *it* was on the mannequin—a Bill Blass suit—way beyond my budget and just begging me to buy it. It was the ideal attire for my attorney's talk. The magnificent suit had a silk crepe pleated skirt, a matching long jacket, and a steep price. But I was in love. As

I swirled around in front of the dressing room mirror, turning it down was not an option.

Once home, I carefully hung it in the back of my closet, never to be touched by human hands until the day of my presentation.

The Big Day Arrives

On the day of the corporate image talk, I slipped into my stunning new suit. Just before my program began, I went to the ladies' room, freshened my lipstick, and admired myself in the mirror one last time before going off to win the crowd.

The first part of the talk went beautifully. About ten minutes into the seminar, however, I turned my back to write something on the flip chart. The crowd gasped. I heard women suppressing giggles. Spinning around, I saw attorneys with smirks on their faces nudging each other. Others turned away embarrassment. The group couldn't hold it in any longer, and laughter broke out all over the room.

The meeting planner came scampering up the aisle like the worried white rabbit. She whispered in my ear, "Leil, your skirt is caught up in your pantyhose." Now it was my turn to gasp. I grabbed at what I thought was going to be the back of my skirt. Instead, my hands landed on bulging pantyhose with my silk skirt trapped under it. I had mooned the venerable attorneys and their staffs!

I attempted to cover it with humor by saying, "Heh heh, you'll notice 'modest' wasn't in my introduction." That weak joke didn't work, so I made a second attempt. I told them that the acronym "C.Y.A." suddenly had a new significance for me. (In the Lawyer's Bible, it stands for "cover your ass.") That one broke the ice. Laughter ensued, and the crowd's discomfort dissipated. But not my humiliation.

It was tough to get back on track with the presentation. I figured I'd better get off of skirts and talk about something else. "Ahem. Jackets are powerful for women," I began. Peeking down at my notes, I spotted a ring of perspiration under my arm expanding like a ripple from a stone thrown in the lake.

"Just don't choose silk," I mumbled.

After I laid that egg, Little Trick #3 was hatched.

LITTLE Trick #3
Do a "Dress Rehearsal" Before Your Important Occasion

Never wear anything new to an important event, interview, meeting, or on a big date. Unless you enjoy snickers and scorn, give your new outfit a dry run when you're on girl's night out or having a beer with the boys.

If I had worn my new suit someplace just once before the speech, I would have discovered silk clings to pantyhose and pitilessly reveals perspiration.

Not for Women Only

Gentlemen, for fashion and safety, you too should try out your clothes before committing to wear them. Single gentlemen, this is crucial because women are ruthless when it comes to judging a man's clothing. One slipped sock showing a hairy leg could get you written off.

Men have told me horror stories of unraveled trouser hems, popped buttons, and zippers that unzipped at inappropriate moments. One gentleman told me his new date heard his howl from the men's room. How could he explain to her that his zipper got caught on a tender part of his anatomy?

Believe it or not, in first-class conservative companies, a man's clothing is even more crucial. To a certain degree, the cut of his suit and shine of his shoes can determine how far he goes in the company.

But what if I'm not going anywhere social to try new clothes out? I'd feel ridiculous pushing a shopping cart in a suit or sky-scraper heels.

Not a problem. Read on.

Home Sweet Home

You know how relaxed you are in your favorite jeans and T-shirt watching TV or reading a book. Tranquility is anchored to these clothes. Each time you slip them on, you feel psychological ease. They are like your second skin. You're not worried that your tee is too tight or your jeans too short. Why? Because you've lived in them.

Now let's talk about your new knock 'em dead outfit. You know you look like a million bucks in it. However, if the outfit doesn't have that comfortable "lived-in" feeling, you won't be at ease wearing it. To make a good impression, you must be relaxed in whatever you've got on your back. Here is a technique to do just that.

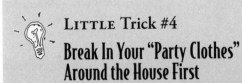

LITTLE Trick #4

Break In Your "Party Clothes" Around the House First

Give your jeans and old sweater a vacation. Don your slick new clothes and run around the house in them. Watch TV in them. Organize your CDs in them. Take a nap in them—especially if they're cotton, so you see how they pass the wrinkle test. After they are cleaned, they will look just as good. And you will look even better, because you won't have that stiff "I'm wearing new clothes" look.

How to Make People Appreciate Your Introduction

No two people hearing the same words—at the same time, from the same person—ever get the same sense of what someone said. Every sound that comes out of someone's mouth strikes a minefield of each listener's buried memories, associations, and a lifetime of emotional pleasure or pain from everyone they've ever met.

Even the order of words in a single sentence can affect how someone feels about the speaker. For example, I've often heard a man introduce his wife: "I'd like you to meet my wife, Wilma." Or a wife say, "This is my husband, Harold."

Most people would ask, "What's wrong with that?" Can you guess? It will be obvious after I tell you about a bigheaded former boss.

Whenever this man introduced me, he would arrogantly announce, "This is my assistant, Leil." Once it was, "This is my assistant, uh, uh, Leil."

The facts were correct. I was, indeed, his assistant. What stung was the order of his words. He said it as though his first four words were the only essential ones, and the last word, my name, was optional. Would it have hurt his self-image to think of me as a human being whom he employed as his assistant—rather than any featherless biped who could fill that role? I wished he'd dismount his high horse just once to predict how the way he worded his sentence made me feel demeaned and disconnected from him. People would have a different impression of both of us if he had said, "This is Leil, my assistant," putting my name first.

Whoa! Back up, Leil. You're being way too sensitive.

My answer is *everybody* is supersensitive—when it comes to themselves.

I'm sure ol' Bighead didn't mean to demean me. He just didn't have the Emotional Prediction that the CEO in the Introduction did.

It's subtle. It's subliminal. It takes superior sensitivity. But it's worth it. Your prediction of other people's feelings makes them feel good, not only about themselves, but about you. They probably won't even be aware of whether their name came before or after their position. They'll just know they feel better when they're around you.

Put Their Name Before Their Position

Don't say, "Meet my *boyfriend*, Harold." Say, "Meet *Harold*, my boyfriend."

Don't say, "I'd like to introduce you to my wife, Wilma." Replace the subconscious pain prick with the pleasure-pat of hearing, "Wilma, my wife."

If it is not something simple like "my wife," stop after saying her name. Then start a new sentence heralding her relationship to you. I dreamed of hearing Mr. Pompous say, "I'd like to introduce you to Leil. She is my assistant who has been working for me for three months."

And, of course, I wouldn't have minded if he insisted on adding, "and I really like working with her." That comment would have made people like *him* more, too. Shakespeare told us, "All the world loves a lover." He forgot to add, "All the world likes a 'liker.'"

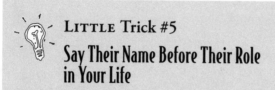

LITTLE Trick #5
Say Their Name Before Their Role in Your Life

Don't flaunt the position someone plays in your life first. Introduce him as a real flesh-and-blood human being who actually has a life apart from you—and even a name to go with it! After giving his name, insert a verbal period. Then, in a new sentence, inform your listeners of the role he has in your life.

Dale vs. Leil

If Dale Carnegie were alive today, he and I would duel with our pens over the next Little Trick. Mr. Carnegie's reputed "hail fellow, well met" philosophy was excellent for the 1930s and for many decades thereafter. In the new millennium, however, many of us have had it up to our ears with hyper types who "come on big." In business and social situations, we respect people who have a more thoughtful approach to conversing.

If you start out too low-key, though, how are they to know how magnificent you are?

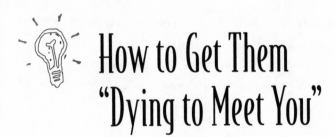

How to Get Them "Dying to Meet You"

You are going to a gathering where there will be lots of new folks. So you brush your teeth, spray on deodorant, shine your shoes, and look in the mirror. You like what you see. But will new acquaintances agree?

Suppose you are not hot or drop-dead gorgeous. What if looks are not your strong suit? How else can you impress them? If you don't tell them about your brilliance, your amazing accomplishments, and your, um, humility, how will they know? But if you do tell them, they baptize you a braggart. If you try to slip it in by saying something smart too soon, they swear you're a show-off. It's a catch-22.

So what's someone like you with a myriad of marvelous qualities and exceptional achievements to do? Enter Little Trick #6.

Have you ever listened to a lecture by some so-called celebrity you never heard of? The introducer exaggerates endlessly about her triumphs and talents. After such an inflated introduction, the audience is salivating to see and hear this highly esteemed individual.

How Does That Help Me?
I'm Not Making Any Speeches

Yes, you are! Every time you open your mouth, you are, in essence, making a speech—especially when meeting someone new. And, like the so-called celebrity, if somebody gives you a great introduction *before* they meet you, you have a primed audience.

Let me tell you how I discovered this Little Trick. A friend in Chicago took me to a meeting at her chamber of commerce. After the presentation, I was talking with a member named Foster, a Hewlett-Packard salesman. While waiting for the coordinators to bring out some snacks, we were discussing food, as hungry people often do.

That was his opening. Foster said, "Leil, I'd like to introduce you to a friend of mine, a chef. I know you'll like him. Roberto does a lot of community work. In fact, he ran in the Chicago marathon to fight breast cancer last year."

Cool! I want to meet this athletic chef who supported breast cancer research.

Would it have been smooth for Roberto to tell me his impressive credentials out of the blue during the discussion? Of course not. Even if Foster had sung Roberto's praise *during* the introduction, it wouldn't have been the same. Hearing about him first from someone else—and meeting him *after*—was the winning combination.

You Toot My Horn, and I'll Toot Yours

I never would have become wise to their game if, a short time later, I hadn't been standing with Roberto and a few men who were talking about—what else?—sports. That was Roberto's opening. "Guys, there's a buddy of mine standing over there who's headed off to Miami for the Super Bowl in a couple of weeks, and he's sitting right on the 50-yard line!" The others were obviously blown away by this marvel. "Yeah, sure," one guy said sarcastically. "Only God sits on the 50-yard line."

"So who does he know?" asked another.

"Nobody," Roberto replied. "He won it for being one of the top ten salesmen at Hewlett-Packard."

Hmm . . . it seems these two guys have a great gambit going.

It was confirmed later when Foster casually brought up the subject of dining, which, of course, was chef Roberto's favorite topic and one in which he could shine. I don't think it was an accident that the owner of a four-star restaurant "just happened" to be standing in our circle—an excellent contact for Roberto.

The two pals really had their act together. Roberto told the guys about Foster's sales honor. Foster brought up Roberto's favorite subject. And what woman wouldn't be impressed by an athletic chef who ran in the breast cancer marathon?

It Also Ignites Conversation

Did you spot the bonus benefit to their little trick? It provided fodder for a myriad of conversation topics: restaurants, being a chef, community work, breast cancer, marathons, winning sales trips, and, of course, football. Need I even mention the advantage for Roberto whenever Mr. Top Restaurateur is looking for a new chef?

Always Give More than You Get

I abhor the philosophy of "tit for tat." I have found, however, that if you give more than you get, it usually comes back to you. And if not, you at least have experienced the joy of giving. In that spirit, let me share Little Trick #6 with you.

Pause now and think about several of your friends. What are some of the really great things they do? Is he in a band, or does he volunteer as a Big Brother to disadvantaged kids? Was she just promoted to chief strategy officer at her company, or did she win the chili cook-off? The next time you are introducing, or about to introduce, your friend, mention those facts.

Bring Up Your Friend's Favorite Subjects in a Group

This is another way to make your friends look good. What are their favorite subjects? Do they get excited talking about music? Astrology? The Loch Ness monster? Championship ballroom dancing? Lizards? UFOs? If you find a way to bring up that subject, your friends can dazzle everyone with their insights. And, of course, it deepens your friendships.

If you have a close friend you can confide in—and conspire with—read on.

Why leave the above to accident? Make a "conversation pact." Agree to tell people great things about each other—and bring up the other's favorite subjects when both of you are speaking with people.

> ### Little Trick #6
> ### Make Your Friends Look Good (and Have Them Do the Same for You)
>
> When you are introducing friends, be sure to put them in a great light by giving more than just their name. Tell something wonderful about them. Even if you both know the group and introductions aren't involved, bring up your friends' favorite subjects so your pals can sound off knowledgeably.
>
> Do this with no thought of reciprocity and watch your friendships deepen. However, if you have a no-holds-barred buddy and are both comfortable with an arrangement, agree to do the same for each other: "I'll toot your horn. You toot mine."

What Is the World's Best Pickup Line?

Gentlemen, you will know the answer to this eternally perplexing question by the time you finish this chapter. Men lay awake at night fantasizing how to impress women. They dream of pickup lines, read books on how to be a player, and practice personality tricks to make them swoon. Some even attend seminars and take online courses.

Fine, I'm sure some of it works. Countless studies, however, including a landmark one published in the *Journal of Research in Personality*, found that one of the most important qualities women seek in men is his being respected, especially by other men. There's no better way for you to demonstrate that fact than by having a male friend tell the woman you're interested in how great you are.

What is the best opening line? Something positive a male friend says about you. In other words, have another man give her your best opening line!

Although most people don't anguish about their first words with a woman as much as single men do, everyone is conscious of the impression her first words make on a group. No matter what she says, her goal is to "prove herself." Even unbeknownst to her, she is subconsciously saying, "Hey, look at me. I've got a good personality. I'm participatory and I'm going to add a lot to this conversation. You will enjoy listening to me."

Unfortunately, many people overdo it. They don't realize this has just the opposite effect.

How to Make Everyone Anxious to Hear Your Opinion

Have you ever attended meetings where one staff member is the first to raise a hand, ask a question, and, a few minutes later, ask another? Before long, the same person makes a comment.

The opinionated employee pipes up so often that the annoyed meeting coordinator finally sputters, "Let's hear from someone else now." Everyone sighs in relief. When a person who hasn't spoken up before shares his opinion, the group is all ears.

One day, several years ago, I was with a small group of five or six people sitting around a friend's pool. Other than a very brief introduction, I hadn't met one of the women, Jan Storti from Sarasota, who seemed to be listening intently.

The group was bantering about everything and nothing, and everyone offered opinions on both. Everyone except Jan, that is. She hadn't said a word. I was curious about how she felt about the various topics, but I didn't want to make her uncomfortable by asking. She might be shy.

Half an hour into our conversation, however, Jan enthusiastically jumped in with a view on what we were discussing at the moment. She happily surprised us with her comments, and we were anxious to hear what she had to say. After that, she contributed a lot to the conversation, and we especially enjoyed hearing her. Why?

Because Jan had been so quiet at first, we had time to build up curiosity about her. We also appreciated her because, retroactively, we realized something special about Jan. Unlike many people who speak up soon to show their outgoing personality, she wasn't out to prove anything. Thus, Jan inadvertently proved to all of us how cool and confident she was.

Are You Shy?

If so, my heart goes out to you. I was unbearably timid right into my early twenties, so I understand. Meeting people was agonizing, conversation was excruciating, and dating was out of the question. I always foolishly felt I needed to prove my confidence immediately. So I would thoughtlessly blurt out something inane and spend the rest of the conversation silently wondering if the others thought I was an idiot.

Up until recently, the public wasn't aware of the vast difference between shyness and introversion or highly sensitive people. The latter take their time processing information. They listen carefully and usually speak more slowly. This is definitely not a lack of intelligence. As reported in *The Journal of Children in Contemporary Society*, 60 percent of gifted children are introverts, and they get higher grades in Ivy League colleges. In many situations, people regard more thoughtful and slower reactions more highly than quick answers.

If only I'd known then what I know now, I would have first listened silently and sincerely to what others were saying. Then, when I did speak up, my observations would sound more reflective. People would be more interested in my comments, and that would help me have the confidence I craved.

Little Trick #7 is not just for pool pratter. It is even more powerful at work. At the beginning of most business meetings or important discussions, let the other participants have their say first. Listen carefully as though you are evaluating each comment before you speak. That gives your eventually revealed opinion more value.

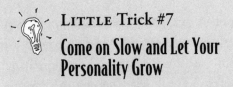 **Little Trick #7**

Come on Slow and Let Your Personality Grow

Don't feel compelled to jump into a discussion right away. When you are quiet at first, you create a sense of mystery. Simply listen to and make good eye contact with the others while they are talking. When you do decide to speak up, your awaited comments carry more weight. Your earlier calm, confident silence becomes, retroactively, impressive.

Three Impressive Ways
to Demonstrate Deliberation

- **When you know the answer.** When someone asks you a question during serious discussions, you don't have to give a quick answer, even if you know precisely what you want to say. Wait three seconds before responding.

  During this time, be sure to keep your eyes focused on the questioner's. It makes a powerful impact because, as Michael Argyle proved in *The Psychology of Interpersonal Behaviour,* confident people who are more intelligent do not find eye contact during silences as disrupting. The intensity doesn't rattle their concentration.

- **When you don't know the answer.** If you don't know how to respond to a question or how to phrase your answer, don't waffle or wing it. Look at your questioner with a slight smile and say, "I'd like some time to think about that." Then gently change the subject.

- **When you don't want to answer.** If someone asks a rude question, calmly use his name, look him straight in the eye, and say, "I don't know how to answer that, Name." Keep a neutral expression, but don't look away.

PART TWO

ELEVEN LITTLE TRICKS

to Take the "Hell" Out of "Hello" and
Put the "Good" in "Good-Bye"

How to Have a One-of-a-Kind, Noticeably Outstanding Handshake

No one disputes that people form a quick opinion of you the split second your image reaches their retina. I disagree, however, with the hackneyed adage, "You never have a second chance to make a good first impression." Someone gets an intense second impression of you the moment your eyes lock and your bodies touch in a handshake. A weak handshake shouts "Instant Disconnect!"

Will Lipton, the former CEO of a very successful company in Greenwich, Connecticut, told me he once faced the tough choice of hiring one of two candidates who were equally qualified for a top position. When I asked him who got the job, he replied, "The one with the better handshake."

Nowadays, most enlightened people know they should not be knuckle crunchers, dead fish floppers, fingertip grabbers, pumpers, or kiss-my-ring shakers. So in the past few years, no one handshake really stood out as special—until last month.

After a speech I had given for GM, Canada, the president and managing director shook my hand.

Whoa, that's one heck of a handshake, Mr. Elias.

It was strong and friendly, and it created a connection I hadn't felt since my Girl Scout secret handshake. I couldn't figure out why his had such power. I had highlighted the importance of handshakes in my speech, so I felt comfortable complimenting his.

Arturo Elias smiled, turned his wrist over, and pointed to the vein where the doctor takes your pulse. "Leil, it's all right here," he said. "Whenever I shake someone's hand, I lightly place my pointing finger on their pulse." In a sense, this is touching the shakee's heart, because a person's pulse is a wave traveling directly from the heart.

I was instantly converted and am now a shameless pulse presser. Recently, a Free Mason told me the group has twenty handshakes; the "Lion's Paw" of the Master Mason involves pressure on a brother's pulse, so it must be big-time stuff. When you get used to it, you will become sensitive to the connection your new handshake makes with your shakee.

LITTLE Trick #8
Press Their Pulse When Shaking Hands

Whenever shaking hands with someone, do not press like you are taking his pulse! But to create an instant connection with a new acquaintance ever-so-lightly place your forefinger on his wrist vein so he feels the warmth of your body flowing into his. Sliding your hand into his far enough to reach his pulse forces your webs to touch, another sign of a great handshake.

# How to Exchange Business Cards with Class

At one of our monthly chamber of commerce meetings, the coordinator introduced me to Gakuto, the head of a Japanese business association. We chatted a bit and then, as people promptly do at such gatherings, he handed me his business card. I glanced at it, thanked him, and put it in my purse. I then gave him mine.

He gently took it and, holding it with both hands, gazed at it as though it were made of fragile Japanese rice paper.

Golly, Gakuto, it's just a business card. You can put it away now.

I must admit, though, I rather liked the attention he was giving it. The way he kept gazing at it made me feel important. In fact, when I broke the silence, it seemed to shatter his concentration. Gakuto pulled his eyes away from my card, almost reluctantly, and we continued chatting.

Out of the corner of my eye, I noticed he was still holding my card with both hands! To me, it represented respect and continued curiosity about my work. I suddenly felt a closer connection to this man who took my card seriously.

He even glanced at it again once or twice while we were talking. Talk about making me feel special!

The Japanese Touch

The Japanese may not be touchy-feely with people, but they sure are with business cards. These polite people call it *meishi*. The word has the cachet of the ceremonial aspect of exchanging cards.

I'm sure Gakuto wasn't thinking of his actions as a "Little Trick." He was simply following the Asian tradition of treating someone's business card respectfully. The Asian culture conveys Emotional Prediction in many of their practices. For example, they have a passionate sensitivity to "saving face."

I figured you don't need to be Japanese to get away with holding someone's business card respectfully with two hands, so I gave it a try. It created an almost tangible connection with the next few people I met.

LITTLE Trick #9
Hold Their Business Card While Chatting

Do not just glance at a new acquaintance's business card and quickly stash it into your pocket or purse. First, hold it with both hands and gaze at it as though it were a small piece of art hand-painted especially for you. Then you can switch to holding the card with one hand, but continue holding it at waist level or just below. To make her feel esteemed and valued, give it a respectful glance from time to time.

A Cool Way to Give Your Card

Just as the choreography of taking someone else's card is significant, demonstrate respect for your own when giving it. You needn't ceremoniously bestow it; neither should you shove it at the recipient like a worthless piece of cardboard stock. I've seen people exchange cards as though they were dirty Kleenexes.

Keep your cards in an attractive card case and handle them carefully. Think of your business card as the Japanese do. You are giving someone a representation of yourself. It shows you take pride in your profession.

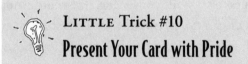

LITTLE Trick #10
Present Your Card with Pride

When giving your card, take it out of an attractive carrying case gently and present it horizontally, with the script facing the recipient. Hold it just a bit higher than usual—not in his face—but at a height where he could almost read it in your hands.

If you respect your work, others will, too. After all, people who love the work they do and do the work they love are the big winners in life.

How to Be a Successful Networking Conversationalist

That same evening, I discovered another big bonus of holding someone's business card while conversing. The coordinator introduced me to a gruff auto parts dealer. As is the custom at these meetings, I handed him my business card. He quickly eyeballed it and stuffed it into his back pocket, which, of course, would be a grave insult to an Asian.

Practicing my new skill, I continued to hold Mr. Auto Parts's card respectfully and glance at it occasionally. Understandably, my not knowing an air filter from a clutch constricted our conversation. And if I told him I was a motivational speaker, his first thought would be the speakers in his car stereo. In other words, we were from different worlds.

Unfortunately, fate—and the coordinator—had sentenced us to struggling with a few seconds of convivial conversation, but neither of us could think of anything to say. We just stood there looking at each other.

To break the awkward moment, I used my brand-new "card trick." Once again I looked at Mr. Auto Parts's business card, which I was still holding in my hands. Bingo! It was pure conversation inspiration. Under his company name, I saw a photo of a circle-shaped gizmo with six little thingamajigs protruding from it. "Interesting card," I fibbed. "What is the picture?"

His deadpan expression suddenly dissolved, and a big smile replaced it. "A distributor cap!" he exclaimed excitedly. Whew, I had inadvertently hit on a subject he was passionate about.

"Uh, and what does a distributor cap do?" I asked. Pretty lame, I know, but it got us through a couple of conversational minutes until we could gracefully split and move on to more pertinent conversation with other people.

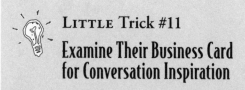

LITTLE Trick #11
Examine Their Business Card for Conversation Inspiration

When talk lags, look at your conversational partner's card again—which, of course, you are still holding. It can rescue you from discussion deadlock. Even if his card doesn't have an interesting photo like a distributor cap, you will likely find a conversational cue in the card—the logo, his title, the mission statement.

Small business owners often design their own cards. There, staring right at you, is another opening for an interesting story—or one they find interesting, at least.

If appropriate, you could comment on an unusual title on her card. During the past year, I have been able to resuscitate near-death conversations by asking what exactly an "electroplater," "phrenologist," and, I kid you not, an "erection coordinator" does. My favorite card had "Top Dog" as the job title.

How to Give—or Avoid—Social Hugs

Most of us have been hugged by people we loathe and left unhugged by people we love. At this very moment, serial huggers are attacking hug haters, while hug haters are hurting hug cravers by not hugging them.

In short, "to hug or not to hug" has become something of a national dilemma, one that can turn otherwise genial greetings into social disaster. I take no stand on the divisive hug issue, but offer instead some hugging hints.

Self-Defense for Hug Haters

When someone approaches you with arms outstretched and a big, glowing jack-o'-lantern smile, it is obvious that you are the intended victim of a hugger. Short of faking a soggy sneeze, there are few defensive moves. You can try to avert the impending embrace by thrusting your right hand out and dangling it in midair as though it were hungry for a shake. Unfortunately, this is an obvious hug evasion technique, which makes the hugger feel instantly disconnected from you. My advice, medical or significant psychological conditions aside, is to grin and bear it. To date, no one ever died from a hug.

Now, a Note for Happy Huggers

Most likely, you are a people person and you sincerely enjoy bodily contact. You wish you were an octopus so you could hug four people at the same time. Many of your fellow embracers tell me a hug is a handshake from the heart. Unfortunately, not everyone agrees.

"So, shall I swear off hugging?" you ask.

No, of course not. But let the other person adjudicate whether to be a Shaker or Hugger. If she doesn't welcome your imminent display of affection, you can usually tell by her body language and, in extreme cases, terrified eyes.

If not, open your arms wide, but keep your elbows close to your waist. If your intended hugee welcomes your embrace, she will slide into your low-slung, welcoming arms. If not, she will grab your right hand, still open at waist level, and shake it—relieved that you are not one of those effusively invasive hugging types.

LITTLE Trick #12

Let *Them* Choose Whether to Hug or to Shake

Pro-Huggers, camouflage your hugging intentions by keeping your elbows almost touching your waist as you open your arms. That permits your potential huggee to make the call of whether to slide into your embrace or grab your right hand and give it a shake or two.

A final word of warning to both camps. Beware of giving or receiving promiscuous hugs too early. Once you have established that you have a hugging relationship, withholding the embrace in subsequent encounters could be confusing at best, cruel at worst.

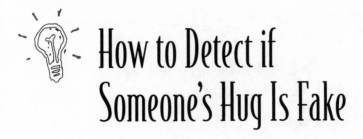

How to Detect if Someone's Hug Is Fake

It is my obligation to alert you that some hugs carry heavy negative emotional baggage. How can you tell?

Ponder for a moment a sincere hug. That's the kind Grandma gives her grandchildren and long-lost friends share when reunited. Both loving spouses celebrating their anniversary and young people discovering the joy of love express their emotions with a sincere hug.

The "I Really Don't Enjoy Hugging You" Hug

There is, unfortunately, a counterfeit category of hugs. It is the kind colleagues at industry conventions (who don't remember each other's names) annually impose upon each other. It is the obligatory kind people give distant relatives they never knew they had at family reunions. And, of course, the kind you see cutthroat competing employees bestow upon each other at the company Christmas party.

What's the difference between the first group of hugs and the second? The distance the huggers stand from each other? Sometimes. The tightness of the squeeze? Usually. But here is where the rubber really hits the road in hugging sincerity.

Uncomfortable Huggers Pat Each Other's Backs!

Say someone throws his arms around you but, a few seconds later, his hands transmogrify into flippers on your back. This indicates he is uncomfortable hugging you for one reason or another, and it mitigates the authenticity of the hug. His hand-flapping discloses discomfort with your closeness.

Do not assume back-patting is always negative, of course. Without knowing the particulars of a relationship, precise analysis is seldom possible. Here are a few situations, however, where people often employ the "Patter's Hug."

- **Two men:** Two gentlemen wish to express friendship, but they want to make it quite clear to each other they are not physically enjoying the hug. How? They thump their hands on each other's backs.
- **Two women:** Mutual back-patting by women also expresses discomfort with the closeness, but it doesn't convey the same fear of misunderstood sexual orientation.
- **A man and a woman:** Now it gets more complicated. Four possibilities follow.
1. If the male and female like each other but are not sexually attracted, they immediately begin patting to convey their erotic disinterest.

2. If one of them would like to take the relationship further, but the other wouldn't, the person who starts patting is signaling lack of sexual attraction, while the disappointed other pats back to show he or she (supposedly) doesn't care.

3. The two are sexually attracted to each other but feel they shouldn't be enjoying the hug so much. So they release anxiety through mutual back-patting.

4. When ex-lovers run into each other, they usually start with a sincere hug. When it dawns on them that the relationship is over (or that their new partners are watching), they start patting.

LITTLE Trick #13
Don't Pat When You Hug

Stay in an embrace as long or as short as the situation and hugging partner warrant. But do not let your hands become flippers on her back lest it subliminally signal that you want to disconnect.

Don't go crazy analyzing it if your cohugger starts patting your back. It commonly occurs when one of the huggers feels the embrace is lasting too long, signifying, "OK, time's up. Let's end this hug thing." When she starts patting, smile and smoothly curtail the hug.

I hope the foregoing hasn't stripped the joy of hugging away from huggers, forced hug-haters to grin and bear agonizing embraces, or made you suspicious of everyone who hugs you—or just plain paranoid about hugs. All I mean to say is: be sensitive to the vast difference in people's reactions to hugs and act accordingly.

Now, I want to give you a safer, one-size-fits-all embracing option. It is a subtle, nonoffensive gesture that clearly says to an acquaintance, "I want to hug you but perhaps it's not appropriate."

How to Show You Like Someone Without Being Forward

One evening at a gathering, I was telling an elderly gentleman a tale that proves cats don't have nine lives. At least mine didn't. Sadly, Sedgwick fell out of a sixth-floor window.

Most males might consider that narrative schmaltzy. But this gentleman's hand reached out to touch my arm in compassion. Halfway, however, it seemed he thought better of it. His arm stopped halfway. He respectfully pulled it back, thus giving me the impression his instinct was to touch me affectionately. In spite of his compassion for my deceased cat, his respect for me won out.

Thus, Little Trick #14 was conceived: simply reach out as though you are going to touch someone, but stop in midair and return your arm to its original position. It is a subtle technique and, when executed innocently, is lovely. You make the recipient feel you revere them, but you don't want to express your warmth in an untoward way.

For Those Who Are in Love— or Want to Be

Men, you can use this move on a female friend whom you would like to make more than a friend. She may appreciate your affection but can't accuse you of being too forward. Needless to say, the only acceptable body parts for the "no-contact caress" are the arm or, on rare occasions, the cheek.

Women, it works wonderfully on men. Their fantasies go wild wondering what it means.

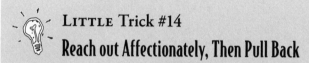

LITTLE Trick #14
Reach out Affectionately, Then Pull Back

Whenever the occasion and desire unite, extend your arm as though you are going to touch someone's arm to express fondness or sympathy. Then, as though realizing the possible inappropriateness of your gesture, pull back. You have now demonstrated affection, respect, and decorum.

A Time to Touch

There are times when you should *not* avoid touching. For many centuries in India, people in the lowest class were called Dalits or "Untouchables," and the upper classes wanted no physical contact with them whatsoever. Salespeople have told me that's how they feel when a customer flings money on the counter for them to scoop up. When paying for something, put the money directly in the salesperson's hand. That and concurrent eye contact silently say, "For this brief second, you and I are connecting."

How to Play It Cool or Play It Hot in Business and Love

All people have finely tuned antennae that subconsciously sense your enthusiasm about meeting them. Especially in a cutthroat corporate environment, people are aware if your energy level is above or below theirs, and by how much. In other words, "Who wants to meet whom more?"

For example, let's say you are a salesperson calling on a potential customer. Suppose you slink in with a smile like a big banana is stretching your lips from ear to ear and say, "THANKS FOR TAKING THE TIME TO SEE ME, MS. BIG DEAL PROSPECT!" What is she going to think?

This guy is frantic to make the sale. If he's that anxious, he must be having trouble pushing his product. Maybe it's too shabby. I better not buy it.

If instead, as you shake her hand, you say a low-key, "Thanks for taking the time to see me, Ms. Big Deal Prospect," what does that signal?

Hmm, this guy looks pretty confident about his product. It must be selling well. Maybe I should try it.

In business, if your eagerness is much higher or lower than the other person's, an essential sense of balance and equality is lost. It creates a much quicker connection when the two of you sound equally pleased to meet each other.

How do you maneuver this? You simply let the other person say the first words and then harmonize with his energy. I know, this is a daunting task for extroverts who are accustomed to jumping the gun on the "hellos." But, under certain business circumstances, it's best to hold back.

From Business to Pleasure

How heartbreaking it is that dating has become a competitive sport—or that it is any type of game at all. In an ideal world, the male and female of our species would spot each other, smile, and feel confident, friendly, and equally delighted to meet the other. Unfortunately, from the second human animals sniff potential romance their hearts shift to high gear and their heads start to spin. Moments later, the mating game begins.

Gentlemen, let's say you spot an attractive woman. You're as edgy as a mouse staring at the cat. But you straighten your tie, tuck in your tummy, and make the move on her. You say, "Hi, my name is . . ." But before you can finish your sentence, she looks at you lethargically, gives a ladylike snort, and turns away. She makes you feel like a flake of dandruff on her shoulder.

The opposite doesn't augur well, either. Say you spot another stunning creature. Same scenario: You go up to her and give her your lively, "Hi, my name is . . ." With twice your enthusiasm she responds, "OH WOW, I'VE BEEN WANT-

ING TO MEET YOU. I'M SO THRILLED YOU CAME OVER!"

Egad, is this girl desperate or what?

If someone acts like meeting you is the most exciting thing that ever happened to her, naturally, you are flattered. But, if she comes on *too* big and gushes over you, your reaction is, *"Hmm, what does she want from me?"* Or maybe, *"Gosh, if she is so overly impressed with me, she must not be very desirable."* It's like when Groucho Marx said, "I don't want to belong to any club that will accept people like me as a member."

The following Little Trick pertains mostly to business and love.

 LITTLE Trick #15

Let Them Speak First and Match Their Enthusiasm

You've heard the axiom, "Dress a little bit better than your customer, but not too much." The axiom when meeting someone in business and love is, "Sound a little more enthusiastic, but not too much."

Be aware, too, that there are times when, for tactical professional reasons, you might want to show a little less eagerness and go a decibel or two lower than your contact.

Happily, strategy seldom comes into play in purely social situations. Be as energetic as you like when meeting potential new friends. And be grateful that you don't need to play those silly games.

Some of my seminar students tell me they feel intimidated meeting and greeting people at a highly professional or society event. The following tip is most assuredly not for meeting everybody. But keep it in your holster to whip out when faced with similar situations.

How to Say Hello to Prestigious People

Everyday scene: Someone says to you, "I'd like you to meet So 'n So." Most of us respond with "Hello," "Hi," or the like. Some folks prefer "Hey, Dude" or "Yo."

I'm not putting that down! Anything more than a casual greeting could sound pretentious, even snooty. But Little Trick #16 is for making an instant connection with people on the top rung of the professional or social ladder. (It also impresses pompous people wherever you meet them.)

How to Sound Highly Cultured

These days, you seldom hear an entire sentence spoken when meeting someone. You'll hear sentence *parts*, like "Happy to meet you," or "Pleased to meet you." But those mutterings wouldn't pass a grade school grammar test. Your teacher would point an accusatory finger at you and demand, "Where's the subject? Where's the verb?"

To make a good impression in formal settings, go for it—an honest-to-goodness whole sentence with a subject, an object, and maybe an adjective or preposition thrown in. For starters, try, "I'm happy to meet you." When you feel at ease with that one, upgrade it: "I'm *very* happy to meet you."

"What a pleasure it is to meet you" counts as a complete sentence, too, although Emily Post would stick up her cultivated nose at the word *pleasure*. Speaking of Emily, here is one for the la-di-da department, but don't toss it out. It will keep you afloat when swimming around in upper-class circles. If a lady says, "How do you do," it is *not* a question! Shame on you if you actually answer, "Fine." Her blue blood would hemorrhage. You merely say the same words back, with the same emphasis, "How do you do." (Not, "How do YOU do?")

Go figure.

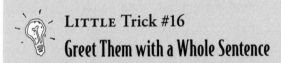

Little Trick #16
Greet Them with a Whole Sentence

When meeting people in highly professional or upscale situations, watch your Ps and Qs. In this context, that stands for periods and question marks. Hit them with a whole sentence that includes a noun and a verb. Adjectives optional.

I repeat, I am not suggesting flawless phraseology and Emily Post's ritual when meeting new casual friends. Keep in mind, Emily died in 1960, and many of her suggestions should be buried with her.

More Shine for Your Act

Every day before noon, you hear greetings like "Mornin'" or "G'mornin'" floating around the office, the neighborhood, or the gym. Suppose you wake up tomorrow morning and say to yourself, "Today I feel like going up a notch or two in people's estimation."

Easy task. To sound smarter, more professional, and cultured, simply pronounce all three syllables of a greeting. "Good mor-ning." "Good eve-ning." It's a no-brainer.

Ah, if only all methods of making a first-class impression could be so simple!

How to Meet the People You Want

I must log this Little Trick under a heading called "The Ignored Obvious." You would think everyone would do it every time they entered a room full of people. Yet in all my years of speaking for groups, I've seldom noticed anyone consciously performing Little Trick #17.

Friends usually sit together in a seminar, so here I'm addressing participants who enter alone. If the first arrival sits in, say, the right rear of the room, the next arrival sits in the left front. The next in the left rear, and so on. Each sits as far from the other participants as possible until all the seats are filled.

During the break in singles' seminars, I often notice a male audience member eyeing a female across the room or vice versa. Now, unless one of them is blessed with that rare quality called complete confidence, they are never going to converse. If only one had chosen a chair next to the other, however, sparks could have ignited.

Ditto in corporate programs. Employees must know the advantage of sitting next to a big cat in their own company—or anyone else in the corporation or industry who could be important to them. But what surprises me is that I never see a participant walk in ten minutes early and wait by the wall to see where other people are sitting before choosing a chair.

Here's the plan: Be among the first to arrive at a large industry, company, or social presentation. However, do not choose your seat—yet. Stand at the side of the room and eyeball everyone who comes in. When you see your target person, pretend the music just stopped in a game of musical chairs. Sprint to the seat next to Mr. or Ms. Opportunity.

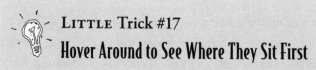

LITTLE Trick #17
Hover Around to See Where They Sit First

If you are seeking any important alliance, arrive early at the gathering and hover around the sides like a helicopter. Then, when you spot that important someone, make a speedy landing in the seat right next to him.

Keep your bodily parking spot in mind whatever you are searching for. Where you deposit your bottom can change your bottom line.

In the first seventeen Little Tricks, we've covered everything from making strong eye contact to playing it cool when necessary.

Using the previous seventeen Little Tricks will give people a great first impression of you. But how can you make sure it will last? Read on.

How to Make a Great Last Impression

You are pacing the waiting room of the personnel department before an interview for an entry-level job in the industry you have always dreamed of. You hear the words you've been waiting for, "Ms. Samuels will see you now." You clear your throat, push back your hair, and mumble a nervous "Thank you" to the receptionist. You're as tense as a turkey in November.

The moment you cross the threshold, Ms. Samuels smiles, stands up, and walks around her big desk toward you with her hand out. She says, "Welcome. Please have a seat. Settling in behind her desk, she says, "I've read your résumé and have been looking forward to meeting you."

Whoa! Your confidence soars. You chat amicably. You answer her questions accurately. The woman on the throne is obviously impressed.

Now you're really flying high.

But as the interview ends, so does her smile. Instead of standing to see you out, she's shuffling through papers. With a disinterested voice and no eye contact, she murmurs, "Thank you for coming. Good-bye."

You crash. Your head is reeling. What did you do wrong? She was so warm at first and now . . . nothing.

Driving home, you feel like a human malfunction.

Much, much later that night, just like a worm regrows the missing part when cut in half, your survival instinct starts mending your severed ego. You wake up the next morning loathing the person who slashed it.

Did Ms. Samuels consciously try to make you feel like a worm? Of course not.

Maybe she had a lot of work to do. Perhaps she had an important call to make. Possibly . . . conceivably . . . feasibly . . . perchance . . . It could be anything. Only one thing is sure. Ms. Samuels was not a big cat.

We have defined people with EP as "being aware of themselves, their surroundings, the current situation, and other people. They make a concerted effort to harmonize all four."

Ms. Samuels lost on all counts.

- **Themselves:** She wasn't sensitive to her role vis-à-vis you. Ms. S. didn't realize you might perceive her as the woman who holds your entire professional life in her hands.
- **Their surroundings:** She didn't sense that sitting behind her big desk across from you was daunting. People who are sensitive to your emotions move chairs so there are no obstructions between you.
- **The current situation:** She knew, of course, that she was interviewing you for a job. But that's where it stopped. Big cats understand the magnitude of the occasion for you. They know the implications of their actions and your possible interpretations.

- **Other people:** Here is where Ms. Samuels really lost it. She was immune to the thousands of signals you gave off—that we all give off—every minute of interacting. She wasn't even aware of the obvious—how tense you were at the beginning and how her smile melted it away. She didn't notice your pride when you answered her questions, nor detect your devastation at her lukewarm dismissal. If Ms. Samuels had had an ounce of EP, she would have sounded equally as enthusiastic, if not more, as she said good-bye. A big cat makes people feel good about themselves, even if they don't get the job.

Why Are People So Obsessed with Their First Impression but Seldom Their Last?

Have you heard of the Von Restorff effect? Hedwig Von Restorff was a German physician/psychologist who proved that the last item on a list has a long-lasting effect. Last impressions are thus almost as memorable as first. Trial lawyers use this Von Restorff effect to set murderers free or send them to the electric chair by saving their most powerful arguments for last.

Motivational speakers punch their pillows at night trying to come up with the perfect finale to their speech—one to bring the applauding audience to their feet.

Take a tip from these pros and pay attention to your passion level as you part, not just when you meet. Keep in mind that, for a big friendship or professional boost, your "good-bye" must match or, preferably, be bigger than your "hello."

Just as a job applicant wants the interviewer to be every bit as enthusiastic at the end of the discussion as at the beginning, we want people to like us even more after we talk to them. If they don't sound as warm or warmer, we suspect we disappointed them in this last contact.

The Origin of Little Trick #18

The technique of leaving a great last impression blossomed from a small seed—a seed that still annoys me like it's stuck between my teeth.

Whenever I'm on a trip, my dear friend, Phil Perry, and I often chat on the phone. I call him when I'm on the road and enjoy his, "Hello Leil! It's great to hear your voice. How are you? How's your trip going?" Lots of warmth. Lots of energy. Lots of friendliness.

As we are ready to hang up, however, his enthusiasm nosedives. He mutters a quick "G'bye." Click. He could just as well be saying, "Buzz off!" He doesn't mean it any more than Ms. Samuels did. It's just that neither understands how a lively hello and a lackluster good-bye affect someone. Subconsciously, they feel they disappointed you.

Verbalizing your delight is even better. Don't leave it to chance. Practice a few upbeat goodies to juice up your good-byes in person, on the phone, or in your e-mail (which we'll talk about in Part Nine). And don't forget to use their name each time. Here are some examples.

Saying good-bye after having met and chatted with someone:

"I really enjoyed meeting you, Marisol!"
"Gian, I'm glad Joshua introduced us!"

Now you encounter a friend or acquaintance on the street or at a party:

"I'm so pleased we ran into each other, Renee!"
"Good bumping into you, Brendan!"

At the end of a meeting or evening with a friend:

"I had such fun talking with you, Tania!"

When you're about to hang up on the phone:

"Gabriella, great talking to you! I'm glad your trip is going well and looking forward to seeing you when you get back."

Incidentally, Phil now gives me a huge "good-bye" ever since I showed him this chapter for permission to use his name.

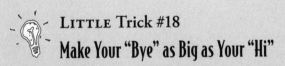

LITTLE Trick #18
Make Your "Bye" as Big as Your "Hi"

The next time you meet someone, make a note of how enthusiastic you sounded when you said hello. Then, when it comes time to say good-bye, boost your energy level up a tad higher. If appropriate, tell the person of your pleasure.

A lively good-bye is like a warm kiss at the end of the evening. A lethargic, low-energy one sounds like a kiss-off.

PART THREE

TWELVE LITTLE TRICKS

to Develop an Extraordinary Gift of Gab

How to Get Lively Conversation Going with People You've Just Met

People with the gift of gab have that Midas touch of being able to say howdy to strangers and chitchat with anyone. Their most noticeable quality is how quickly they connect with the dozens of people we all encounter daily—salesclerks, ticket agents, taxi drivers, telephone operators, fellow elevator passengers, and a whole world of others. Long animated conversations with people they've just met seem effortless. When you too are adept at turning these strangers into acquaintances (and those you fancy into friends), you'll know you are a graduate in the gift of gab.

"But what shall I talk about with these strangers?" you ask.

Psychiatrists have an annoying habit of always answering a question with another question. So I'm giving myself a promotion now, and Dr. Lowndes will do the same. My answer to your question is this question: "What is everyone's favorite subject?"

Right, it's *themselves*. But you already knew that. You continue, "But, if I don't know them, I can't just say, 'Hi, tell me about yourself.'"

True. However, let me tell you how one stranger got me talking about myself in spite of the miserable mood I was in. In one hour, she transformed me from a stranger to a friend. I'll always be grateful to my long-distance pal, Cheryl Mostrom, for inspiring this next Little Trick, which you can use with anyone you meet, anytime, anywhere.

How to Turn a Grumpy Stranger into a Gabber

One icy February day five years ago, I had a predawn flight from New York to Phoenix for a speech. At 4:00 a.m., I contemplated hurling my sadistic alarm clock out the bedroom window. But, lest it rub out some passerby, I decided against it.

There was no time for breakfast at the airport, and these days an "airline meal" is an oxymoron. A howling infant and his mom were my seatmates, so sleeping was not an option. As I watched the flight attendant pass out one puny packet of peanuts per passenger, I considered filching the jar of pureed apricot from the kid's baby bag.

Changing planes at Midway Airport, I raced to the connection gate a good half mile away—just in time to sit on the plane for an hour while they deiced the wings. After a bumpy takeoff, the flight attendant passed out barf bags instead of peanuts.

The Arrival

As often happens, the event coordinator, whom I hadn't yet met, picked me up at the airport. Meeting planners usually ask the obligatory, "How was your flight?" before moving on to grill me on every aspect of the program I've planned for them.

This time, Cheryl, from the law firm Fennemore Craig, who up until then was just a slight phone acquaintance, said, "You must have gotten up terribly early this morning. What time did your alarm go off?" She then inquired whether I'd had time to eat at the airport or if they served anything on the plane. On our walk to her car, she asked questions like, "Were the gates close together in Chicago when you changed planes?" "Was there much turbulence?" "Were you able to sleep on the plane?"

It was as though Cheryl had been filming me since the moment I staggered into my predawn shower. Had she seen me racing through the airport corridor at breakneck speed? Did she feel me itching to hurl my shoes at the security man who made me take them off?

I was flabbergasted at her sensitive queries because she only knew three facts: I took an early flight; I had to change planes in snowy Chicago; and the flight was an hour late. From those few clues, Cheryl envisaged what I'd gone through and realized I would want to get it off my chest. She demonstrated Emotional Prediction (EP) at its finest, and I felt an instant bond with her.

If Cheryl hadn't asked those on-target questions as she drove me to the hotel, I would still have been grousing silently about my miserable trip. Instead, by the time we got there, we were both laughing about "the flight from hell." I would have performed my entire speech in the car for her if it would have set her heart at rest that it was right for her group.

After I got to know Cheryl better, I complimented her on her insight about my experiences before I arrived. She said, "Leil, it's the same thing you did when you sent me your preprogram questionnaire." A preprogram questionnaire is a list of questions speakers send to clients so they can get to know the organization better before speaking for them. One of the crucial queries on the questionnaire is, "What has the participants' day been like up until the speech?"

I haven't seen Cheryl, who lives two thousand miles away, after that day we met five years ago. But we have remained phone and e-mail friends ever since.

A Surefire Technique Get a "Great" Conversation Going

Little Trick #19 is based on an irrefutable phenomenon in nature: *Anything up close looks larger than when it is at a distance.* This is true for experiences as well as for objects. For example, I didn't feel Cheryl's questions about my alarm clock or the proximity of the airport gates was small talk. Not at all. These hassles were still a big deal to me. I enjoyed getting them off my chest.

Here is the technique to get interesting conversation started—at least interesting to the other person. When you first meet someone, you know next to nothing about him. With very little effort, however, you can find out some trivial facts about his day. It can be as simple as asking someone at a party where he lives. If he lives at a distance, ask about his long drive. Ask questions like, "Was there much traffic?" "Were you driving on a highway or country roads?" "What's the speed limit on those roads?"

It may sound silly to you, but this is not "small" talk to him. Why? Because details are still on his mental windshield. The time proximity makes them loom larger than they really are.

Inquiring about the traffic and speed limit the next day would seem trifling, even weird. But, at this moment, it is relevant conversation for him.

Questions about someone's last few hours just kick-start the conversation. Soon the natural flow takes over and one subject leads to another. Take any seed of information you've gleaned. If you plant and nurture it, you will be amazed how quickly it turns into an animated discussion.

It Works Wonderfully with Friends, Too

It's Wednesday. Your friend knows what time she woke up. What challenges she faced at work. Where she had lunch, what she ate, and with whom—and lots of other forgettable stuff.

To you or any of her other friends, these facts are diddly-squat. However, they played a significant role in her Wednesday. That evening, she will love talking about them. By Thursday, she has forgotten Wednesday's details, so asking then would sound pandering and foolish. For good conversation, catch someone's trivia while it's hot! Little Trick #19 isn't just for creating conversation though. Since good friends are the only ones who talk about trivia with each other, chatting about your new acquaintance's minutia gives the cachet of already being closely connected.

Soon after I discovered how well this Little Trick works on acquaintances and friends, I decided to see if it also works on people you see all the time, like a family member or someone you live with.

The high price of real estate in New York City necessitates some unusual living arrangements, so I have a male friend (Phil

Perry) as a roommate. (I call him my "platonic male room-mate." He says we're "friends without benefits." Same thing.)

Phil likes to take long leisurely walks through the city on Sunday mornings. When he returned from his next walk, I asked him dozens of tiny details, anything I could think of. "Phil, how was the temperature?" "Did you see many people on the street or was it deserted?" "Were there many stores open?" "Did you stop for breakfast?" "Where?" "What did you eat?"

He didn't find my queries strange. He loved talking about his just-completed stroll—so much that I had trouble changing the subject.

 LITTLE Trick #19

Ask People About Their Last Few Hours

To get a new acquaintance (or an old friend) talking, ask about her day, preferably the past five or six hours. Visualize as many details as you can and ask about them. As far-fetched as it seems to you, she's loving it because she is so close to the experience. Each particular question has a short shelf life, so use it while it's hot.

The formula is simple, and the conversational payoff is huge.

How to Start a Friendship with Complete Strangers

Naturally, if you have time to spend with someone after being introduced, you can more easily lay the foundation for a friendship. In today's fast-paced world, however, that's a tough task. Say you have a quick conversation with a receptionist at an organization you're visiting and you'd like to get to know her better. Or you meet a man at a gathering who works in tech support at a nearby company. But your time to make a connection is short. Turning your brief acquaintance into a friend is a challenge. However, if you plan it well, the following technique accomplishes just that.

Soon after saying hello, bring up a subject, *any* subject, that you could logically follow up with another question. For instance, ask for nearby restaurant recommendations, driving directions, where to buy something. Ask her which movies she suggests. Get his advice on which home computer you should buy. Think of something that you just might "need" more information on later.

Asking for recommendations is good for two reasons. You could have "forgotten" what movie she suggested and have to call again. If you followed his recommendation about a computer, it is reasonable to contact him again to ask where you should buy it.

Find a logical reason to contact the "previous stranger" a third time. After seeing the movie or buying the computer, call to say "thank you" for the excellent advice. In the case of the receptionist, you could even stop in to thank her in person.

The secret is making those follow-up contacts. They promote you from stranger to acquaintance. You are now in a better position to make him or her a friend.

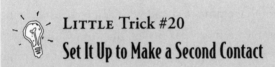

Little Trick #20
Set It Up to Make a Second Contact

Get your acquaintance talking about a subject that has a logical follow-up question. Then contact her again for further information. As long as it relates to what you talked about, there is nothing strange about getting in touch a second time—or a third. Now you are on the path to friendship.

The Next Step

If you would like to orchestrate a friendship where you do things together, use the second or third conversation to get your new acquaintance talking about his interests. Then find a related situation that could involve an invitation. Does he like theater? Indian food? Horror movies? After several short phone conversations, your invitation seems logical.

Even better is relating the activity to your initial conversation. The receptionist told you she loves movies? There's your opportunity when a new one opens. The techie who recommended your computer would be pleased if you "just happen" to have two tickets to the technology expo when it comes to town.

Incidentally, I am not concentrating on dating here. A myriad of other factors, which I cover thoroughly in my book *How to Make Anyone Fall in Love with You*, are involved creating that kind of special relationship. We're primarily talking friendship now.

A Fun Little Trick for Going from Stranger to Acquaintance

Noah Webster (the dictionary guy) never came across a common word that practically every twenty-first-century person knows—at least those in the northeastern United States. It traces its roots to a Germanic language that developed in the tenth century.

Curious? Drum roll, please. The word is *schtick* (sometimes spelled *stich*, *sticth*, *stitch*, and lots of other ways, depending on the geographical and religious roots of the user). *Schtick* is defined as a "contrived bit of business, often used by performers." I am not talking about your Uncle Charlie's schtick of spinning a plate on his finger or pulling a quarter out of your ear. I'm referring to a more subtle, spoken schtick that has the power to make people smile, lift their day, and feel an instant connection with you.

Many people we see daily are in service professions, such as the cashier at your favorite coffee shop or the counter person at Taco Bell. Employees serving the public often plow through their day feeling anonymous and nameless.

Here is how to brighten their day and practice your gift of gab at the same time: give people a schtick-name. A schtick-name is similar to a nickname, but you create it from a pleasant experience you've had with that person. Or it can just be a flattering nickname.

Let's say you know the Italian word for "beautiful" is *bella*. The cashier at your regular coffee shop is Italian-American. You can get her day off to a great start hearing your cheerful "Ciao, bella" (Hello, beautiful) in the morning.

At Taco Bell, you always order a half-pound beef and bean burrito with cheesy fiesta potatoes. One time, the guy at the counter started preparing this delicacy the minute he saw you. Your schtick can be calling him "Kreskin," the famous mind reader.

I have a schtick-name for the receptionist at my doctor's office. One time I had a sharp pain in my neck, a real one, not the kind some people give us. I called my doctor's office and asked to speak to Dr. Carter. Camille Mazziotti, the receptionist, answered. As I was describing the pain, she asked me very astute medical questions.

Then she said, "Of course, Leil, the doctor can call you back. However, she's with a patient now, and I know what she might suggest. May I tell you?"

"Sure, Camille." I followed her advice, and the soreness disappeared. So what is the schtick we both have fun with? Every time I speak with her, I call her "Doctor Camille." I know she enjoys the professional promotion, and I enjoy making her smile.

The WIIFM (What's in It for Me) Factor

As with most of the Little Tricks in this book that enhance people's self-esteem, there is something nice in this one for you too.

Let's go back to the coffee shop. Whoops, you left your wallet home today? "Bella" is not going to insist you pay for it now (or maybe ever).

Darn, today at Taco Bell there is an unusually long line. Well, "Kreskin" might just work his magic. He'll place your order the minute you walk in the door.

Incidentally, "Dr. Camille" always finds a way to fit me into my doctor's fully booked schedule.

What About Your Friends?

It's not just the English who go bonkers over titles. Everyone loves having one. Does your friend Patrick teach you things? Call him "Professor Patrick." Does your friend Stefanie do good things for people? She is "Saint Stefanie."

Depending on his qualities, your buddy John can be "Sir John," "Father John," "Prince John," "Master John," or "Captain John."

Your friend Linda can be "Lady Linda," "Lieutenant Linda," "Sister Linda," or "Princess Linda."

Their honorable titles are only limited by your imagination and by the qualities your friends would love to have recognized.

LITTLE Trick #21
Give People a Schtick-Name

If you think someone will enjoy it, give him a flattering nickname. It makes you memorable and, at its very least, gives you both a smile. There is one fundamental schtick statute, however. It must augment the recipient's self-esteem.

How to Never Hesitate Starting or Joining a Conversation

A neighbor often brings her twelve-year-old daughter to stay with me for a bit while she's out doing the millions of things most people don't realize a mom has to do.

Kelly is a sweet kid, but she always dons a muzzle around others her age. One afternoon, she was whining to me about an all-girl birthday party she had to attend.

"Why don't you want to go, Kelly?"

"I dunno. I mean, like, I never have anything say."

"Well, what do you think the girls will be talking about?"

"I dunno."

"Has anything happened at school they might be talking about? Think hard, Kelly."

"Well, the school says they're gonna put the boys and girls together in one gym class rather than separate like they are now."

"How do you feel about it, Kelly?"

"I don't think it's a good idea."

"Why not?"

"Well, boys are better at sports than we are, and I don't think it's fair to make us play with them."

"Any other reason?" I asked her.

"Ye-ah. There's this one boy I really like. I don't want him to see me in a dumb gym outfit. My legs are too skinny."

Hooray! I had talked Kelly into verbalizing an opinion about the situation.

The following week, I asked Kelly if she had enjoyed the birthday party. She said she had a blast and spent the next ten minutes telling me about the great discussion they had on that "dumb gym class idea."

I smiled, secretly taking credit, because I had made Kelly articulate her attitude ahead of time.

Become Opinionated!

Many people think just *knowing* current events or happenings is sufficient to keep up a conversation. Not by a long shot! Conversation isn't just giving a newscast. You must have an *opinion* on each issue to be able to speak up and be interesting.

Have you heard of a position paper? It is an essay that presents a stance on an issue. Politicians would be afraid to open their mouths without one.

Celebrity managers write them for the latest luminary when she gets caught snorting cocaine. Or the latest heart-throb so he can explain why he's a Tibetan Lamaist. Or the football player so he'll know what to say about steroids. Why are we any different?

Don't wait until a particular subject comes up and noodle your opinion on the spot. By the time you think of what you want to say, they'll be babbling about something else.

Before being with people, read the top articles in today's newspaper. Think about a popular movie or TV show you saw. What type of people does your group talk about? Sports figures? Movie stars? Politicians? Ask yourself how you feel about each issue or person. "Write" your own position paper.

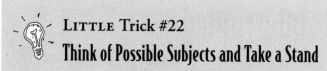

LITTLE Trick #22
Think of Possible Subjects and Take a Stand

We do it before a business meeting, so why not for social gatherings? Make a list of possible topics people might discuss. Now imagine a TV interviewer asking you in front of a million viewers, "So, tell us your thoughts on such 'n such." Be prepared to astound the nation with your shrewd insights.

An additional advantage of preforming your opinion is that when you concentrate on a current event, you'll find yourself becoming somewhat passionate about your position. Thus, you will be inspired to *start* a conversation about the subject. That, of course, is a big part of the gift of gab.

In fast-paced conversations, it's hard to get a word in edgewise. People possessing the valuable gift of gab go with the fast flow of the conversation but still manage to make their point. The next Little Trick teaches how to do that.

How to Make Your Point When You Keep Getting Interrupted

Several years ago, it was impossible to walk through town without seeing the faces of Angelina Jolie, Brad Pitt, and Jennifer Aniston—or various combinations of the three—all over the newsstands. (For those readers wise enough to avoid celebrity gossip, Pitt left Aniston for Jolie.) In spite of the media overkill, I found myself with a group of friends discussing the love triangle.

At the time, Aniston and Pitt were still together, so the world had hope. But when the speculation turned to the unthinkable, actual divorce, the discussion heated up.

Everyone was cutting off each other's words. It was hardly noticeable though, because we were enjoying one of those fun, fast-paced exchanges that friends have.

A woman named Petra who was new to our group said, "Jennifer should have . . ." But someone jumped in with her opinion before Petra could finish. At the first pause, Petra made a second attempt, saying the very same words, "Jennifer should have . . ." Again, she didn't get to finish her argument. After about a minute, she tried a third time, "Jennifer should have . . ."

Hearing her precise words the third time made us painfully aware that we had interrupted her. It also made it obvious to everyone that Petra hadn't kept up with the conversation and just wanted to say the same thing she'd tried before. This awareness brought the discussion to an awkward halt as everyone turned politely toward Petra to give her the opportunity to have her say.

Petra's point was about as insightful as a pet rock—though, admittedly, this was not an evening when any of us had astute observations. When she finished, everyone courteously waited to see if she wanted to say more. Only then did they pick up the lively exchange with its regular cadence.

The way Petra handled it was a lose-lose situation. Because she introduced her point the same way each time, the group thought, rightly, that she was obsessed with her one point. Additionally, she made everyone feel guilty for interrupting. Essentially, Petra's use of the identical phrase each time ruptured the give-and-take of a good energetic exchange.

Please do not misunderstand. This Little Trick does not justify interrupting people. That is disrespectful, rude, and offensive. Good conversationalists realize communicating, like music, has a wide variety of tempos. There is an enormous difference between a slow-paced, contemplative chat and a fast, impassioned discussion. This particular evening, interruption was not the grave sin it is in normal dialogue.

How Could Petra Have Make Her Point and Still Saved Face?

Petra's mistake was prefacing her point with the *identical* words each time. It made her sound fixated on saying one thing rather than following the conversation. However, she could have retained the group's respect and still made her point if she had jumped in with a different introductory phrase each time.

For example, the second time she tried, she could have started with phrases like these:

> "Many people have a different opinion, but mine is that Jennifer should have . . ."
> "Considering the situation, don't you think that Jennifer should have . . ."
> "I know the tabloids went crazy, but don't you think that Jennifer should have . . ."

That way, if she were cut off again, the group would never know Petra was going to present the identical point she had attempted five minutes ago.

LITTLE Trick #23
Give a Different Preface to Introduce Your Same Point

Sooner or later (and probably sooner), someone is going to interrupt you. So as not to sound like you are perseverating on the same idea, preface your point with different words the next time around. Your listeners will never guess you were going make your original point. Old wine in new bottles works every time.

How to Make Friends with Those Who Don't Speak Your Native Language

One of my short-term roommates, until she found her own apartment, was Sandi Fiorentino, who came to New York to pursue a career in modeling. At five-foot-ten with natural platinum blonde hair that most models would dye for (pun intended), the prestigious Ford agency scooped her up. Sandi was ecstatic because her first shoot was on the Italian Riviera, where she could practice the language she'd been struggling to learn from her Italian grandmother.

When she returned from her trip, she breathlessly told me all about it. Naturally, I asked the question every unmarried female asks another, "Did you meet anybody interesting?" Now Sandi could have met the ten most fascinating women in Italy, but, as every female knows, "anybody interesting" translates into "any interesting men."

Sandi smiled coyly, "Giancarlo. I mean he is supercool, awesome."

"How did you meet him?"

She giggled. "He picked me up on the beach."

"Wow, Sandi, he must have been really hot!"

"Well, no, a lot of other great guys tried. But I couldn't understand a word they said. But for some reason I understood Giancarlo perfectly, and we wound up dating every night. When he comes to visit me, I'll introduce you."

The Hot Italian Arrives

When I met Giancarlo, I mentioned that Sandi told me he was the first man she understood speaking Italian. He winked at me and said very, very slowly, "Parlo . . . molto . . . lentemente . . . per . . . gli . . . stranieri." Even with my abysmally fractured Italian, I understood he was saying, "I speak very slowly to foreigners."

Go, Giancarlo! The fast movers on the beach didn't get the gorgeous girl. The slow speaker did. He understood how people feel when they don't understand a language they're trying to learn.

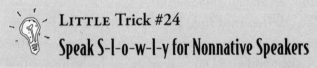

LITTLE Trick #24
Speak S-l-o-w-l-y for Nonnative Speakers

In our increasingly global society, you will meet more and more people for whom English is a second language. For them to understand you, you must slow your speech down—way down. Of course it will sound strange to you. But I promise it won't to your listener. To connect with non-native people, you need to learn a new, very simple language. It's called Really, Really Slowly Spoken English.

# How to Tailor Your Talk to Your Listener(s)

I once spoke at a conference in a less advantaged section of Mississippi with a prominent black speaker, Diana Parks. She is a dynamic woman who is beautifully spoken. So, during her presentation, I couldn't believe my ears when I heard her say things like "He don't know" and "They done it."

After our speeches, I tentatively broached the subject with her. She just laughed and said, "Leil, I grew up here. These are my people. They relate to me better that way." I guess she was right. My speech had bombed, and Diana had received a standing ovation.

It wouldn't have been appropriate, of course, for me to try to speak like Diana. In retrospect, however, I realize I should have edited my talk somewhat to avoid using any unusual words.

It was so obvious—after the fact. "When in Rome, *speak* like the Romans." I felt ashamed of not having predicted the emotions of audience members who didn't understand some of my so-called "big words."

Sometimes You Should Leave Your Big Words in the Dictionary

If you're a five-syllable kinda guy, cut your words to fewer than three syllables in certain crowds. You will make your listeners a lot more comfortable. For example, if you're having a fight with an average Joe and you tell him not to "prevaricate because his argument is specious," you'll get a blank stare. Maybe a punch in the gut. Translate the above into his language: "Don't try to pull that on me. I know what you're saying is crap."

It's similar to what you would do with a kid. If you are talking about, say, cartoons, you wouldn't ask, "Do you like the anthropomorphic ones?" You'd get a blank stare. Maybe tears. Instead, ask, "Do you like cartoons where the animals talk and act like people?"

A study published in the *Journal of Psychonomic Science* showed that if you are "above" someone else—in this case, in linguistic ability—anything you do that "brings you down" to his level makes him feel closer to you.

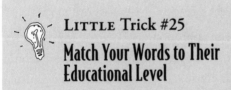

LITTLE Trick #25
Match Your Words to Their Educational Level

Diversity isn't just race, color, and creed. It's linguistic, too—even though it is all the same language. If you want to instantly connect with people, tailor your vocabulary to your listeners, whether it's one person or one thousand.

How to Talk to Less Advantaged People

On average, people make three aborted takeoffs on a career before getting off the ground and reaching a cruising speed with one they like. Single-handedly, I probably jacked up the average from three attempts to twelve.

One of my ditched efforts was as a travel writer. I had fantasies of mountain trekking in Thailand or lying on the beach in Belize—all for free. After querying many publications, I finally received a response from a supermarket tabloid. It didn't matter to me that it wasn't a literary publication. I didn't care that my stories would be sandwiched between recipes for squash soup and how to survive Saturday at the mall with the kids. I had a *travel* assignment!

The editor sent me a contract and the list of destinations I could explore on their dime. I anxiously tore open the envelope. The choices were:

Atlantic City
Disneyland
Niagara Falls

The Grand Canyon
Yellowstone National Park

You've got to be kidding. Where is the Mayan Riviera, Bali, Pago Pago? The places I've read about in *Town and Country*, *Atlantic Monthly*, and *Destinations* magazines?

I raced to the phone and asked my editor if there were any other more, ahem, "unusual" spots.

She said, "Leil, we have to stay within the parameters of the possible with our readers. Most of them couldn't afford to go to the Caribbean, let alone any more exotic destinations."

Roar of thunder, flash of lightning. I got it! She was so right.

I had shown an abysmal lack of EP. I still eat my heart out when I finger through upscale magazines in my dentist's office and see exotic vacation spots I could never afford. (Apparently my dentist can.) I suddenly had more respect for that supermarket tabloid.

And just as the editors understood the lifestyle of their readers, we should understand the lifestyle of whomever we're talking with.

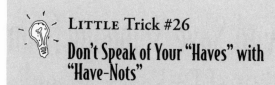

LITTLE Trick #26
Don't Speak of Your "Haves" with "Have-Nots"

Never talk about a luxury that would be unobtainable for the person(s) you are communicating with. Whether it's a vacation spot, second home, expensive restaurant, or a housekeeper, predict their emotions when they hear about something in your fortunate life that will probably never be part of theirs.

Many "necessities" of life to the middle class are unheard-of luxuries to those in less privileged circumstances. Why remind them? Why distance yourself further? Keep your differences a secret, and celebrate your similarities.

Giancarlo, Diana, and my magazine editor had EP. They perceived how badly someone would feel not speaking English fluently, having a limited vocabulary, or living on less money. Well, here's how an anonymous mom's EP saved me from a different kind of distress—total humiliation!

# How to Save Someone from "Dying of Embarrassment"

I want to hug all the people who have saved me from self-recrimination. Hundreds of them!

My most recent salvation was several months ago on a train. I was trying to sleep, but I heard a kid behind me making a ruckus with a video game. Rather than just asking the mother to confiscate it, I figured I should make friends with the little loudmouth first and then make my request.

I turned around. The noisy kid with shoulder-length brown hair had her nose buried in the game.

"Hi," I said, "what game are you playing?"

"Tomb Raider," she mumbled almost inaudibly, without looking up.

I pictured ghouls ransacking graves. "Gee, that's nice," I lied. "Do all the girls in school play these games?"

She looked at me as though I were from a different planet, then at her mother, and dove back into the game. I asked her mother, "What's her name?"

Ignoring my question, the mother smiled and jumped in with, "Yes, practically all the kids have PlayStations. It seems like they're addicted to them." Then, she added apologetically, "They are quite noisy, though. We'll turn it off for a while."

Mission accomplished! Smiling, I turned around to sweet slumber.

When I awoke, I got up to go to the restroom. As I was about to enter the bathroom, a boy wearing a baseball cap with Robert written on it came out. "Excuse me, ma'am," he said in an unmistakably male voice.

On the way back, I passed the noisy kid's seat. Sitting in it was the same brown-haired kid wearing the Robert cap.

"Argh! Her daughter was a son!" I realized. I snuck back into my seat humiliated.

Her Emotional Prediction Tried to Save Me

In retrospect, I realized Robert's mother had that priceless gift, EP. After I had mistakenly said, "all the *girls*" and "What's *her* name?" she didn't reveal her kid's true gender by saying "Robert." She knew how embarrassed I'd be and covered my obviously flawed question by quickly telling me about the popularity of the games. I wanted to hug her.

We've all laid an occasional egg—mispronounced a word, called someone by the wrong name, obviously displayed our misunderstanding or ignorance, said something totally inappropriate or just plain dumb. When someone is guilty of that, you will see by his agonizing expression that he wants to die. You feel terrible for him, but mercy killings are illegal.

The following may not be the most delicate analogy, but it is right on target. If you have ever passed gas when you were chatting with a group of people, you know that one second's silence seems like an hour. Project how the mortified person who passed verbal gas feels. Make a rapid comment to cover his humiliation.

 Little Trick #27

Conceal Their Verbal Blooper with an Instantaneous Comment

If the speaker says something that she may soon realize is mistaken, mispronounced, or just plain dumb, quickly jump in and cover it. Say something distracting *rapidly* so there is little time for it to dawn on her that she's been a dimwit.

Speaking of changing the subject . . .

How to Smoothly Change the Subject

How many times have you been stuck in a conversation in which people are talking about something you know nothing about, care nothing about, or find just plain BOR-ing? But you can't jump in with a new topic out of the blue. It would sound weird. So, how do you change the subject to something more interesting without sounding strange?

First, let's explore the logical progression of conversation. Practically everything anyone says comes from free associating with something that the last person just said. Here's the pattern:

1. You make a comment that obviously relates to what Person X just said.
2. After that, Person X (or Y) picks up on a point related to what you just said.
3. You do the same again, and on it goes. It doesn't sound weird because your listener(s) understand the connection between the two thoughts. The pattern continues whether you are a group of two or twenty. In this way, one subject gradually and logically flows into another.

But that's too slow for you! You want them to get off the current topic and change the subject *now*.

Here Is the Little Trick

If you want to discuss a specific subject, pick up on something (a thought, a phrase, or even just a single word) the last speaker said. Repeat or rephrase it, and then relate it to what you want to say. If you invoke their thought and then link it, even loosely, to yours, the connection makes sense to the listeners.

For example, do you want to talk about a recent movie you saw? Or your new horseback riding lessons? Maybe you want to tell them about the great renovations you're doing to your house. But, darn, they're talking about the most tedious subject in the world, the weather.

Let's say some wearisome woman complains about the downpour last Saturday. Another adds, "It's dreadful. It's raining every weekend." Now your challenge is to go from (snore) rain to the movie you enjoyed. Here's how.

In your first sentence, allude to rain. In your next, connect it to your desired topic. For example, "On *rainy* weekends, I usually go to a movie. In fact, just last week I saw one called . . ." The transition sounds smooth to people because *you* mentioned rain and then said something related to it.

If you prefer to talk about horseback riding, say, "I sure hope it doesn't *rain* next Saturday, because I have my second riding lesson. . . ."

You want them to know about your home renovations? "I'm praying it does *rain* next weekend, because, instead of taking the missus shopping, I'll have an excuse to stay home and keep working on the new rec room." Each time, you only had to say the word *rain* to logically link it to your desired subject.

Changing the subject is a time-honored trick for politicians. Listen to any Sunday morning political TV talk show and count the number of times they pull it off!

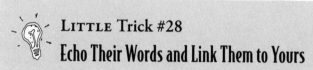

LITTLE Trick #28
Echo Their Words and Link Them to Yours

To change the subject, repeat or rephrase the most recent speaker's words or idea, then tie it to yours. If you include or allude to what someone just said, people won't even notice that you've changed the topic!

Of course, there are many times when you should *not* change the subject, no matter how boring it is for you.

How to Know When to *Never* Change the Subject

One of my consulting clients instituted a new inventory control system and gave the entire company training on it. Nevertheless, months later, most of the employees were still stumped. All except one, that is, a quiet nice-guy geek named Günter.

During one of the company's casual round-table meetings, the CEO announced that Günter had graciously offered to coach anyone who needed extra help on the new system. As Mr. Santos continued singing his praises, I peeked at Günter. He was self-consciously looking at his lap, but I could tell he was bursting with pride, reveling in his boss's compliment.

Santos continued, "I'm sure everyone is already grateful to Günter. Several people have told me that, whenever they had any trouble with their computer, Günter would drop whatever he was doing and . . ."

Before Santos could finish his sentence, however, one of the other employees jumped in with, "Well, some of the positions where the new computers have been put aren't really convenient. For instance . . ."

While the interrupting employee, Devin, droned on, the rest of Günter's compliment was forgotten. By all except Günter, that is.

He had been savoring his verbal kiss until the man with mental myopia cut his kudos short. If Devin had had a trickle of EP running through his veins, he would never have cheated Günter out of the rest of his well-deserved recognition.

Actually, it wasn't Günter who lost the most that day. Should Devin's computer crash a few weeks later, how rapidly do you think Günter would rush to his aid?

It's Not Just for Compliments

Not switching topics goes for many more situations than just when someone is being praised. Always keep your EP tuned in to those around you. If you notice the subject of the moment is extremely enjoyable to anyone in the group, slap on the muzzle.

Let's say you, Sara, and a few others are sitting around someone's living room. The group is discussing Sara's kids, Sara's vacation, Sara's anything else she especially likes talking about. No matter how boring the discussion is to you, do NOT change the subject. (Let someone else do it. Sooner or later they will.) Let Sara savor the current conversation until it dies a natural death or someone else does the dirty changing-the-subject deed.

Predict Sara's displeasure if the subject abruptly gets changed—and her displeasure with the person who changed it.

LITTLE Trick #29

Never Change a Subject Someone Else Finds Special

Never change the subject or leave when you sense the conversation is important or special to someone in the group. Especially if others are verbally applauding that person, let the last note of the accolade sink in. In fact, don't even be the first person to speak postcompliment, unless it is to add your own refrain to their hymn of praise.

Not so incidentally, even if you are not part of the conversation, don't leave the room during their "thrilling" repartee. It's tantamount to walking out on them personally.

How to Not Give the Same Answer Twice

When I was speaking at a convention last year, a potential client asked me where I grew up. "Washington, D.C.," I chirped, and we moved on to other conversation. Five minutes later, she asked me the same question: "Where did you grow up, Leil?"

Ouch! How should I answer? If I repeat the name of the city, she'll remember she asked before and feel dreadful.

There was no escape. When I meekly mumbled, "Washington, D.C.," she winced at her own error. From this point forth, she would subconsciously anchor me to her own embarrassment.

It's *Their* Gaffe. So What Can *I* Do?

This brings us to the question, How should you handle it when someone asks you the same question twice? You certainly don't want to humiliate him. I brooded over this, to no avail. But a month later, the answer came to me from on high—literally.

I was flying to New York from Denver. During a conversation with my seatmate, I discovered she also lives in New York City. I asked her, "Where in Manhattan do you live?"

She responded, "At 82nd Street and Park Avenue," and we went on to other subjects. Ten minutes later, I asked her the same question: "Where do you live in Manhattan?" Cheerfully and without missing a beat, she answered, "Right across from the Metropolitan Museum of Art." She then *quickly* asked me if I'd ever been there. I told her yes, and we continued our chat until we touched down at JFK airport.

Several weeks later, I wanted to see a new exhibition at the Metropolitan. Just before leaving my apartment, I rechecked the address: 82nd Street and Park Avenue.

Hmm, where have I heard that recently? Lightbulb over head. That's where my seat partner on the Denver flight lives.

It all came clear. Her cool maneuver saved my being mortified. The first time I asked where she lived, she said "82nd and Park." When I asked again, she told her absentminded seatmate, "Right across from the Metropolitan," which just happens to be at 82nd and Park. At the time, I didn't connect her two answers. Not hearing the same words rescued me from the humiliation of having asked before. She had obviously predicted my emotion—that I'd feel like a schnook if I realized what I'd done.

As I walked to the museum, I was hoping I'd run into her to thank her for giving birth to Little Trick #30.

The key to this trick is to never use the same words to answer a question a lousy listener asks twice.

For example, someone asks you, "Do you have a long commute to work?"

You answer, "Not bad, it's about twenty minutes." A few minutes later, Forgetful Asker inquires, "How long does it take you to get to work?"

The only forbidden words for you are "twenty minutes." Respond, "Well, I can be at the office in less than half an hour if the traffic isn't too bad."

Suppose even later in the conversation, Double-Forgetful Asker says, "Do you have a long commute to work?" Give it one more shot to preserve his self-esteem: "A little over a quarter of an hour."

The fourth time he asks, give up and go talk to somebody else.

 LITTLE Trick #30

Use Different Words the Second Time You Must Answer the Same Question

Save someone's face (and possibly her friendship) by responding to her repeated question with different words. Then quickly continue the conversation so she doesn't have time to register her fumble. If she happens to recall her blooper later, she will remember you with gratitude because you swept her embarrassing forgetfulness under the rug.

PART FOUR

TEN LITTLE TRICKS

to Actually Enjoy *Parties!*

How to Make Friends at a Big Party

How many times have you heard (and probably said), "I hate big parties where I don't know anybody." Plastered partygoers with lampshades on their heads have sputtered those same words. Even those in the stylish champagne-toasting crowd assert their aversion to big receptions.

However, if you ask these folks if they like intimate little gatherings where the guests know each other, it's a different story. "Oh, yes, I love those." "They're loads of fun." "Awesome."

Well, guess what? Even the biggest blowout starts out as a small party. I came upon this astounding verity quite by accident when I had to attend a large Sunday afternoon gathering where I didn't know anyone. The invitation said three o'clock. Planning to be stylishly late and thereby diminish my discomfort, I arrived at the hostess's doorstep at 3:45 by my watch and rang the bell.

"Oh, Leil, do come in," the hostess said graciously, but obviously hiding irritation. Then she told me the last thing a partygoer wants to hear. "You're the first to arrive."

Arrrrgh!

She led me into her huge living room. "Just make yourself comfortable. I'm going to finish a few things in the kitchen."

Sure, I'll be comfortable. Ha!

Looking at her clock, I was horrified. I'd forgotten to set my watch back on this first day of daylight savings time. It was only 2:45.

A few minutes later, the doorbell rang. From the foyer, I overheard the hostess say, "Brent, I'm so happy you could come."

A male voice responded, "I apologize I'm here so early. I figured I should get an early start, but there was no traffic coming over."

"It's a pleasure to see you anytime. Let me introduce you to Leil. She was the first one here."

Brent and I started chatting and, much to my delight, he and I really hit it off. As other people arrived, I felt like I was attending one of those "awesome" little gatherings where everybody knows each other.

Soon people started coming in droves, and it turned into what I used to call a "dreaded bash." This time, however, it was different. I already knew a lot of people, the other early arrivals. If I found myself feeling lost and lonely, I had my new friends, the other early birds, to talk to.

Since they introduced me to their friends, like the ripple effect, my circle of acquaintances became larger and larger— and all because I'd forgotten to change my watch. It was a lucky mistake. I'll never be "fashionably late" to a gathering where I don't know many people again.

> ### LITTLE Trick #31
> ### Be Unfashionably Early
>
> Every big function starts out as a little affair. So grit
> your teeth, swallow your instincts, and go early. Be
> among the first to arrive and you will meet everybody
> who's already there. As the party gets bigger, you will
> have a group to hang with and to introduce you to
> other guests.

Attention, Moms and Dads

When Judith McCarthy from McGraw-Hill, the most wonderful editor a gal could ever have, read this, she wrote one of
those cute little pink comment balloons that editors plaster all
over writers' drafts:

> Leil, this is so true. I once mistakenly went early
> to a family party with my kids. I sheepishly said to
> the hostess, "I'm very early, aren't I?" My kids and
> her kids played and I helped her get the food out. It
> went much better for my kids than if we'd arrived
> on time.

And Judith should know. She's a three-time mom.

If you and your progeny are going to a gathering where
there will be other kids, this Little Trick benefits your tots,
too. No child wants to hear, "Now, Rachael, go play with that
rambunctious mob of kids over there."

A Postscript for Shy People

As a recovered Shy myself, I know how arriving early goes against the grain. My mantra used to be, "Slip in late and sneak out early." Shys, I beseech you, try going early to a party just once. You'll see how much more comfortable the whole party will be.

Unfashionably Early Inspired Another Little Trick

Have you ever stood on the sidelines wishing your outfit matched the wallpaper so no one would notice you? Or, worse, been trapped alone in the middle of a laughing, talking throng with a drink in a plastic cup and a plastic smile to match? When a partying passersby smiles at you, you assume she's smirking out of sympathy because you have no one to talk to.

A friend, Ebony, and I once arrived fashionably (but not beneficially) late to a gathering. Both she and I knew only about three other guests, though fortunately not the same ones. Walking in the door and confronting the unfamiliar crowd, I had an epiphany. I asked Ebony to introduce me to absolutely everyone she knew, and I would do the same for her. In addition, we agreed to introduce each other to anyone we met at the party. It worked beautifully!

LITTLE Trick #32
Make a Cross-Introduction Pact

If you don't know many people at a party, make this pact with a buddy: "Friend, I'll introduce you to everybody I know or meet, and you do the same for me."

You might think this is obvious and will happen naturally. But I assure you, unless you sign a verbal treaty, it probably won't.

Using this Little Trick, you will eventually meet everyone there. Do the arithmetic. (I couldn't, but a mathematics professor, drawing on actuarial calculus, combinations, and probabilities, did it for me and assured me it was true.)

How to Meet the People You Want in an Unusual Way

At the beginning of a party, people will be straggling in one by one or two by two. Some of the loners will zip toward their friends like metal shavings to a magnet. Those folks are not your target for this Little Trick. The twosomes, threesomes, and foursomes who strut confidently in aren't, either.

Some lone arrivals, however, will creep in with that pasted-on smile that reveals anything from minor insecurity to major terror. Surprise these hesitant folks by giving them a big smile as they enter. They will figure that you either know them or you are dazzled by their magnificence. Either misunderstanding melts the snow and shovels a clear path right to your vicinity. When they arrive, they may not have the self-assurance to actually put their hand out and introduce themselves. But they will welcome your doing the deed. Think about it. If you were shivering in the doorway of a roomful of strangers, wouldn't someone's smile warm you?

LITTLE Trick #33
Smile at Individuals Entering Alone

The minute they walk in the door of a party, give loners a sincere smile, the crow's-feet kind that reaches your eyes. If they come over immediately, say, "You look just like a good friend of mine. In fact, when you entered, I thought that's who it was. By the way, my name is . . ."

Even if they don't make a beeline directly toward you, be assured that, like moths being drawn to a flame, your warmth will make them want to meet you.

Some of you may think the following Little Trick is wacky. I assure you, it's been road tested by friends who have generously agreed to be guinea pigs for my perverse research.

Skeptical about this one? A friend of mine, Donna Vincent, from New Jersey is currently dating one of her doorway victims. She later told him what she did, and he doesn't mind at all. In fact, he proudly recounts the tale to his friends.

How to Never Look Lost and Lonely at a Gathering

At one time or another, most people have one of the top five recurring nightmares: falling in space, failing a test, running and getting nowhere, being menaced by a monster, and getting caught naked in public.

But practically everyone has this *day*mare: You attend a gathering where guests are laughing, drinking, and making merry. All the while, you're standing alone, looking forlorn and lonely. You fear everyone thinks you are stupid, desperate, fraught with anxiety, and craving human contact.

You may remember my friend Sammy the salesman from my last book. He introduced me to a bizarre technique that has the power to rescue you from the "lonely-among-the-crowd" syndrome.

An organization I had spoken for invited me to an anniversary party and said I could bring a friend. Now Sammy isn't exactly my type. He's a little rough around the edges, but he's got "street smarts" and is a lot of fun. Besides, I hadn't seen him in a while. When I invited him, I warned him he probably wouldn't know anyone there. Sammy didn't mind. He said,

"Leil, the combination of you, free grub, and a couple of beers is irresistible." I think it was a compliment.

The party was in full swing when he arrived. I spotted Sammy at the doorway and signaled him over. As he leisurely wound his way through the crowd, he waved at a few people across the room and gave them a big grin.

By the time he got to me, I was dumbfounded. I said, "Sammy, I had no idea you knew so many people here!"

"I don't," he shrugged.

"But . . ."

"The waving bit? Oh, I've been using that old trick for years."

"You mean you're waving at strangers as if you know them? Don't they think you're batty?"

"Nah," he said. "All that waving and smiling makes me feel as confident as a peacock. Besides, I'm not waving to real people. I'm waving to empty spaces between them. Nobody can tell. They think it's somebody standing behind them or next to them. If I see somebody I like, though, sometimes I'll wave at the real person."

"Come on, Sammy, they'll think you're nuts!"

"No, they won't. They think it's their fault and they should know me. Either that or they assume they're the *only* one I made a mistake on and I really do know all those other people."

The whole scheme sounded outrageous to me . . . until I saw how well it worked. A couple of people he'd waved to gravitated like sheep to Sammy the shepherd. So did some social climbers who had seen Mr. Popularity entering. These determined folks just had to know anybody who knew every-body—and Sammy sure looked like he did.

Little Trick #34
Wave to Imaginary Friends

When you face a daunting swarm of strangers, don't stop at the door with that terrified "Oh no, I don't know anyone here" expression—and then slip in with the speed of a handicapped snail. Glide right in and gleefully wave either between bodies at imaginary people or at a real person across the room. It gets you into the crowd looking popular and confident. And that makes you *feel* popular and confident.

Additionally, when you go up to people, they will be pleased that such a popular partygoer has chosen to speak to them.

How to Ask Great Conversation-Starter Questions

Getting a good conversation going with strangers at a party can be like starting a car in below-freezing temperatures. It takes a couple of discordant attempts before it's up and running. If you've ever found yourself in a situation where no subject seems to turn the engine over, try the next few tips.

When you are speaking with a couple, whether they are on their first date or married fifty years, a guaranteed heart-warmer is, "How did you two first meet?" After giggles or gales of laughter, you will see the joy in their eyes as they recount their first rendezvous.

Some of these stories are surprisingly R-rated! It is delightful to hear the over-sixty set "confess" to their "shameful" (by the standards of their day) first encounters.

The second query is quite simple. The perfect time to pose this question is soon after you have learned your new acquaintance's line of work. Simply ask, "What is your typical day like?" It throws the ball in his court so you can just sit back and listen. Ask friends this question, too. They'll be delighted you care.

Two other surefire conversation igniters are "How did you decide you wanted to become a (whatever their job is)?" and "Why did you choose (name of city) to live in?" *How* and *why* are great words to kick-start a conversation and get it humming.

Little Trick #35
Ask Never-Fail Fun Conversation Starters

Stop for a second. Think back to how you and your significant other met. Wouldn't you enjoy telling the tale? Likewise, would you be pleased that someone cared enough about your typical day to ask? Use these as conversation starters with new acquaintances. If you need more material, throw in a few *how* and *why* questions about their life.

I still regret I missed my big chance to ask that electro-plater, phrenologist, and erection coordinator, "What is your average day like?"

How to Save Face When You've Forgotten a Name

I would like to share another Little Trick I've used with surprising success. Well, moderate success. It won't magically restore your missing memory. But it sure can pluck you off some sticky flypaper at parties.

You are chatting with a friend at a gathering when you spot good ol' What's-His-Name approaching.

Uh-oh, what IS his name? Ouch! He's coming toward me! I'll have to introduce him.

You feel like a fly trapped under a glass, and you sense an imminent case of panic disorder. It's too late to bail out. You bite the bullet. "Uh, I'd like you to meet, umm, uh, forgive me, I'm terrible with names."

That trite alibi makes What's-His-Name feel like the world's most forgettable character, and you have just demoted yourself to a disinterested dimwit.

Wait, It Could Be Worse!

Now you are in the middle of a conversation with someone you know, even a good friend, but suddenly you suffer namenesia.

Her name has completely slipped your mind. (The sixty-plus crowd says it happens quite often.) You calmly surmise . . .

But I'm not worried, I won't have to use her name because I'm already talking with her.

So you and your friend, What's-Her-Name, continue chatting—until someone else approaches. Now your mind races . . .

I'll be superhumiliated. I have to introduce my friend, and I forgot her name. I could just die.

Do not run. Do not suddenly fake a coughing fit. Face it. You've forgotten one or both of their names. Guilty. Case dismissed.

Take heart. Here is relative salvation from these two shameful states of affairs. Energetically chirp to the newcomer, "Hi, how great to see you! Please come join us. Why don't you two (or three or more) introduce yourselves?"

Admittedly, it is not an elixir and it doesn't claim to cover your memory lapse. Everyone sees right through your ploy. However, if you are cool about asking them to introduce themselves, it won't injure their estimation of you. In fact, they'll be thinking, "Pretty cool. I must remember to use that one."

LITTLE Trick #36
Tell Them, "Please, Introduce Yourselves"

Without missing a beat, ask What's-His-Name and You-Know-Who to introduce themselves. Don't kid yourself that you're kidding them. Your ruse is as obvious as a cockroach in a sugar bowl. But they'll secretly admire your style. Confidence in carrying it off is the name of the game here. Think of it as a song where the lyrics are pathetic but the music is hot.

Needless to say, if circumstances ever force you into the sadistic social situation of having to present four or more people to someone, don't even start. You're bound to screw up by the third name. Pass on that and go directly to "Please, introduce yourselves."

What if I Forget Someone's Name Right Away? (i.e., I Wasn't Listening)

Before we leave the all-too-common name-forgetting plague, let us address another common challenge. You have just met someone and, thirty seconds into the conversation, it is as though you never heard their name. You can't ask it again. If you do, you are not only confessing to a Lilliputian memory, but they'll take it as testimony to the fact that they made little or no impression on you.

Question: What to do?

Answer: At the end of the conversation, say something like, "It's really been great talking to you. Once again, my name is _____." Then give a somewhat expectant look without actually asking their name again.

Ninety percent of intelligent life on the planet will take it as a cue to respond with their name.

A Smoother Way to Ask Their Name

I've always admired those confident types who can simply go up to someone and say, "Hi, my name is _____. What's yours?" As much as I advocated that approach, I was never completely comfortable saying it.

Then, several years ago, a woman I had never seen came up to me at a reception. She held out her hand and said, "Hi, my name is Jennifer Newport, *and* yours . . . ?"

Bam! I had an epiphany of the secular kind. Jennifer's substitution of one little word changed her demeanor from invasive to inquiring. Jennifer was just one of those thousands of people in our lives with whom we only communicate for a few seconds. However, I'll always remember her with gratitude for giving me Little Trick #37.

Saying "and" instead of "what" is as different as midday from midnight. By asking "and yours?" you are merely suggesting they finish the sentence you started. It subconsciously preps people for a seamless one-sentence exchange of monikers.

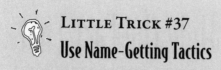

LITTLE TRICK #37
Use Name-Getting Tactics

If you forget a name within seconds of hearing it, remind them of yours and follow it up with an expectant look. Now it sounds as though you want them to remember your name, and chances are they will return the favor. The fact that you forgot theirs doesn't vanish with this Little Trick. You are still culpable. But the fact fades a shade or two.

When approaching people, don't say, "My name is ————————. *What's* yours?" Say, "My name is ————————. And yours?"

Here's a bit of final advice that is superior to all of the above. But it's a lot harder too: just remember their name.

How to Hide the Fact That You Haven't a Clue What They're Talking About

Don't tell me it hasn't happened to you. Everyone is discussing a celebrity, politician, or somebody you don't know but whom you fear is famous. They laugh gleefully whenever someone adds yet another wise insight or heartwarming anecdote about this esteemed individual. And you haven't a clue who this person is.

Whenever you face this daunting situation, use a pretty slick Little Trick a friend from Chicago, Robin Dawson, showed me. She had invited me to the opening of a private library specializing in American history books. Robin and I found ourselves in a circle of literary types, sipping their champagne and discussing William Manchester. My thoughts raced. . . .

Manchester? Manchester? Sounds like everybody should know who this esteemed dude is. But—gulp—I have no idea. Should I ask? No, I'd sound dumb. Should I fake it? No. Because if it becomes evident later that I'm clueless, they'll think I'm a ditz.

I decided that if I listened real hard, maybe it would dawn on me partway through the conversation who he is. But nothing gave me a hint. I feared it was only minutes before my ignoble ignorance would be revealed to all. I'd lose any speck of status with this cultured crowd.

I was relieved when Robin nudged me, indicating she was as clueless as I. Then Robin tapped the person next to her and whispered something to him. They stepped aside and spoke softly for a few seconds. When they returned, Robin leaned over and murmured in my ear, "Manchester was a historian in the second half of the twentieth century. He wrote about twenty books on the Kennedys and lots of other stuff."

"Whew! Thanks, Robin," I whispered back.

At the time, I was just thanking her for the heads-up on Manchester. In retrospect, I was also thanking her for Little Trick 38, which I have used to save face countless clueless times.

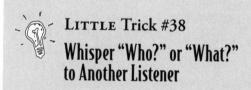

LITTLE Trick #38
Whisper "Who?" or "What?" to Another Listener

When you are trapped in the sticky situation of not knowing who or what the heck everyone is talking about, pull one person aside and confide in her. Ask for information on what or whom they are discussing.

Don't worry that this individual will think you are naive. She will be more honored you chose her for the consultation—and, incidentally, impressed by your tactic.

Whether you're job hunting, friend seeking, spouse searching, VIP schmoozing, or pursuing prospective customers, it is
important to mingle and meet as many people as you can. But
what if some bore corners you and won't let you go?

How to Get Away from Nonstop Talkers

Have you ever known people whose idea of a conversation is a filibuster? You fantasize them suddenly coming down with a case of lockjaw, but no such luck.

You're at a gathering and one of these nonstop talkers decides to hold you hostage. There are other people you want, or should, talk to, but escape seem hopeless. Your left and right brain have a conference to decide how to handle it.

> Right Brain: *I could pretend I have to make a phone call.*
> Left Brain: *Nah, he'll never fall for that hackneyed old song and dance.*
> Right Brain: *I know, I'll say I have go talk to a friend.*
> Left Brain: *You've got to be kidding! He'll see through that in a heartbeat.*
> Right Brain: *OK, so I'll say I need to get another drink.*
> Left Brain: *Uh-huh, Dummy, your glass is already full.*
> Right Brain: *Well, I'll gulp it down and then say I have to get another.*
> Left Brain: *Then you'll look like old guzzle guts. Besides, you'll get wasted. Think harder.*

How to Get Rid of Hardcore Bores

Extreme talkers call for extreme measures. If it's a fairly crowded room, count on your imaginary friends to get you out of this stressful situation. While Time-Hogger is talking your ear off, wave to an imaginary person over his shoulder. Then turn back to Big Mouth: "Excuse me, you were saying . . . ?"

Let him drone on for another twenty seconds. Then peek over his shoulder again. This time, pretend to be annoyed by your "pushy friend" signaling you from behind his back.

The third time you look over Time-Hogger's shoulder, say, "Excuse me, a friend is saying he must tell me something right now. I'll catch up with you later." If appropriate, a friendly touch on the arm substantiates your sincerity. Then disappear into the crowd.

It sounds far-fetched, but I promise that it works. I have never had a Big Mouth turn around to see who is signaling me.

Now for the Honest Approach

This is my all-time favorite way to tackle this situation. Suppose you really were talking to a good friend but knew you must meet other people at the gathering. You'd probably say, "Hey, girlfriend (or guy friend), I love talking to you, but we really should meet some other people now. Catch ya later."

To escape a bore, give her the formal version of this. Tell her, "I really am enjoying talking to you, but we should probably mingle a bit now." She may be as happy as you to do that. Or, if you really want to lay it on thick, say, "I should let you go now. I know there are other people who would like to talk to you. We can catch up later."

Fat chance.

LITTLE Trick #39

Pretend Someone Is Signaling You Over Their Shoulder

Whether your party goal is finding new business, love, friendship, or just some fun, do not let anyone monopolize your time. Either escape (with the help of an imaginary friend) or be (almost) honest and tell him you both should mingle. You—and a lot of other interesting people—have put too much effort into going to the event to get hijacked by an Extreme Talker.

How to Deal with VIPs at Social Events

Did you ever wonder why you seldom see top dentists, doctors, attorneys, stock brokers, and leaders in other respected fields at commonplace bars and pedestrian parties? They like to laugh, drink, dance, and be merry as much as anyone else. Yet many prefer to travel in their own circles. Is it because they are snobs? Most of them aren't. But somebody might make the same gaffe I did. They just can't take the chance.

The chance on what, you ask? The chance that little cats will twitch their whiskers and line up to mooch free advice. I know a dentist who was asked to inspect a partygoer's back tooth covered with cheese and gin; a chiropractor who was beseeched by a tipsy guest to adjust her neck at a bar; and a doctor who was begged to come to the back room so a drunk partygoer could drop his trousers and ask about a mole on his butt. I kid you not.

Doctors, dentists, and lawyers are not the only ones that people try to squeeze freebie information out of. People hit on car mechanics, plumbers, cooks, and hairdressers all the time. These folks are trained specialists who have worked hard and paid dearly to develop their craft. So do not stand with a drink in your hand and ask them how to install a distributor, clear your dishwasher's drainpipe, deep-fry doughnuts, or how to change your hairstyle. They all have business cards and won't turn down your money when you come to see them Monday morning.

I Plead Guilty

Beat me, master. I am a reformed sinner. Yes, I abrogated Little Trick #40 and probably suffered some professional or personal banishment from it. I will never know.

I wasn't aware I had something called a meniscus in my knee until I injured it hiking one day. Doctors define it as a "tear of the anterior cruciate ligament involving the posterior horn of the medial meniscus." I define it as "ouch."

Several weeks after the injury, I was at a gathering. The hostess told me one of the guests was an orthopedic surgeon.

"Great, can you point him out?"

She did. I hobbled across the room and ambushed him by the buffet table. After thirty seconds of small talk, I hit him with my burning question: "Should I have an operation on my knee or live through the pain?"

I detected he wasn't delighted with my query. He handed me his card and said, "My staff will be happy to make an appointment for you." He turned away and found the stuffed crab on crackers more appealing than my conversation.

I'm a slow learner. An hour later, I got a similar reaction from an attorney whom I asked about rent control of a friend's apartment. She suggested my friend make an appointment with her. She shoved her card at me and sprinted off to talk to some more sensitive person.

The hostess never invited me to a party again. Wonder if there was any connection?

You wouldn't go up to a billionaire at a party and say, "You've got lots of money. I'm sure a few thousand bucks wouldn't mean anything to you. So fork some over." Have mercy—and a little Emotional Prediction. That billionaire probably worked twelve-plus hours practically every day year-round, developing the skill to turn pennies into dollars. And you want some free?

"Professional Courtesy" Means "Lay Off"

Every successful person with a trained skill rightfully treasures her talent like a billionaire values his bucks. Her expertise is her fortune. Do not ask a professional to give away her fortune for free. Those mortifying memories of my intrusions hurt worse than my meniscus incisions.

LITTLE Trick #40
Let Pros Party in Peace

Professionals deserve time off, too. People pay for their skill, knowledge, and training. Why should they give it to an information-moocher? Not to mention the liability issues.

You wouldn't ask a magician to tell you how to do his favorite card trick. Likewise, do not ambush specialists outside of their office and ask professional advice. The only permissible question is, "May I have your card?"

It works the other way, too. If you are the professional and someone tries to filch some of your expertise, graciously give him your card and say, "Of course. Call me for an appointment."

PART FIVE

FIVE LITTLE TRICKS

to Handle Invitations: The Good,
the Bad, and the Bummers

How to Increase the Chances of Someone Saying "Yes" to Your Invitation

After I bought my last car, I stayed in touch with the salesman. I stopped in Sal's dealership one day to say hi, and he told me about an interesting tactic that, he said, "everyone in the biz uses."

After the pitch, a car salesman does not ask, "Well, do you want to buy it?" Instead, he places a pen in the prospect's hand (between their thumb and forefinger, with the point facing down, naturally, to make it easier to sign the contract) and nonchalantly drawls, "Will you be taking the blue one or the green one?" "By saying it that way," he told me, "I close more sales."

Similar wisdom pertains if you want someone to accept your social or business invitation. If you ask Ms. Big Shot, "Are you free for lunch Wednesday?" it is a breeze for her to say, "Sorry, busy Wednesday." However, if you cheerfully inquire, "What day might you be free for lunch in the next two weeks?" Ms. BS would have to be a sharp fibber to wriggle out of that one.

Even better, tell her, "I'd like to have lunch with you sometime. Give me a few dates you might be free." Now that's confidence speaking! Between the lines, you are saying, "Of course you want to have lunch with me. I am merely giving you a choice of when."

Incidentally, gentlemen, when asking for a date, the tired old "How about Saturday night?" riff practically begs rejection. Try, "I want to check out the new El Romantico Restaurant. What night are you free to come with me?"

It's tough for a nice lady to say "Never!" She knows a guy's sensitive ego translates that into "I despise you, I can't stand to breathe the same air as you, and I never want your mug reflected in my eyeballs again."

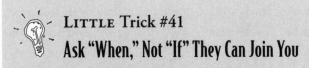

Little Trick #41
Ask "When," Not "If" They Can Join You

When inviting a heavy hitter or a hot date to share a few hours with you, expand the window of opportunity. Do not tie your quarry down to a specific date. It's tougher to refuse if you give him or her the choice of *when*.

Let's turn the tables now. Suppose you are the highly sought-after guest.

How to Turn Someone Down While Retaining His or Her Affection

Someone calls to invite you to a business event, a barbecue, a beer bust, a two-person get-together, or any situation you would rather eat worms than attend. If you don't want to offend the asker, employ the following Little Trick to allay his suspicion about your lack of enthusiasm.

When he first asks you, do not give excuses and refuse. Predict his emotions in this situation. What will happen if you turn him down immediately? In addition to his regret that you cannot come, he will fear that you are rejecting him personally. Your refusal gives his self-esteem a flogging.

Here Is the Plan

Accept that invitation gleefully! Turn your enthusiasm dial to high. If it's a party, ask directions to the fabulous affair. Ask if there is anything you can bring. Ask the dress code. If it's just the two of you getting together, ask about the restaurant, the film, the whatever, with exuberance. Stretch it out as long as he's loving it.

Whether you realize it or not, you have now given the inviter an important part of the pleasure of your company. You make him feel acknowledged, accepted, and approved of. Additionally, you bestow upon him the bliss of babbling about the upcoming date.

At this point, you have two choices:

1. Say, "Let me put it right down in my calendar." Make the sound of ruffled papers. Then return to the phone crestfallen. "Oh no! That's the date I have to go to (fill in the blank). I am so disappointed." He will be, too, but not nearly as much as if you'd turned him down immediately.
2. Accept with pleasure. Then wait an appropriate length of time before calling again. On this call, tell him that you didn't see something-or-other on your schedule and sadly can't make it.

Don't feel guilty! You have rescued him from paranoia as well as given him a valued gift—your apparent esteem.

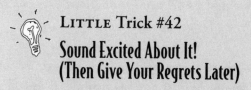

LITTLE Trick #42

Sound Excited About It! (Then Give Your Regrets Later)

When a not-so-liked person extends an invitation to a not-so-liked event, accept it with enthusiasm. Get her bubbling about the date. Only later do you "discover," regretfully, that you can't make it.

Manipulation? Yes, for a very good cause—preserving someone's self-esteem, a quality everyone needs and deserves.

Ladies, if You Want Him to Ask You Out Again

Savvy singles, you have probably already realized how to use this Little Trick in dating.

Ladies, let's say a man you sincerely *do* want to see again asks you out for a particular evening, but you really are busy that night. Do not turn him down right away. Never underestimate the fragility of the male ego when it comes to women. Once burned, he may never ask again.

Accept his invitation eagerly, as above. Now he knows you do want to go out with him. Shortly after, be devastated to "discover" you had something on your schedule. Bat your eyelashes as you suggest, "But some other time . . ."

Now suppose you are not the invitee, but the inviter. Have you ever extended an invitation to someone and afterward hit your forehead . . .

What was I thinking? I don't want to be with this person. I must have been suffering temporary insanity.

I have.

Unfortunately, there is no painless way to get rid of unwanted invited guests, at least not one that's legal. But the calamity did give birth to the following unique Little Trick to make inevitable bummers a lot better for both you and your guest.

How to Handle an Unavoidable Bummer

You've heard kids bawling, "No, I don't wanna to kiss Aunt Ellen." "Don't make me go to Grandma's!" "No, I don't want Uncle Chuck to come. I *hate* him."

That is not just a child's cry of anguish. Adults can feel that way, too. We know, however, that we have to be more "civilized" (read: "hypocritical") about social obligations.

Several years ago, I got a sweet little suite in Sarasota to escape the New York shivers from time to time. On our monthly girls' night out with a few friends and acquaintances, I lifted my one-too-many glass of wine high and, in a moment of euphoria, slurred, "Sara-shota ish is beautiful. I'm going there for Thanksgiving and if any of you want to, hic, come visit, please do." Gratefully, my friends were wise enough to know it was just the gushing of a proud new property owner, not a serious invitation. All except one.

The following day, I received a breathless call from Nina, the newest and youngest member of our group. "Oooh, Leil," she cooed. "I told my boss about your invitation, and she gave me two extra days off at Thanksgiving. I can visit you in Florida!" She paused, waiting for me to share the exhilaration of spending the holidays with her.

Oh poop! There go my plans of sleeping, swimming, catching up on some work—and solitude.

"Oh, gosh, Nina, that's wonderful."

She sensed the lack of exuberance in my voice, because she added, "Well, I mean, if Thanksgiving is the least bit inconvenient . . ."

I was trapped. I felt like a turkey surrounded by a band of hungry Pilgrims. "Oh, no, Nina. It will be so much fun," I lied.

The nerve! Wasn't she worldly-wise enough to know that 90 percent of houseguest invitations are just formalities? Make that 99 percent if someone has had anything to drink.

But I couldn't blame Nina. She got me fair and square. Ol' big mouth here had invited her, and Nina's only crime was taking me seriously.

You Mean I Can Get Rid of Unwanted Guests?

You are facing two challenges here. One, you want the Uncle Chuck or Nina types in your life to feel welcome (even though they aren't). Two, you want to relax during your together time and not have to be constantly on guard that your true feelings will slip out. Psychologists tell us that, no matter how you try, you can *never* hide it if you are harboring hostility. They call it "emotional leakage." If Unwanted Guest asks for something extra, a supposedly "unseen" frown will flicker across your forehead. If he sneezes, your "God bless you" will sound more like "Go to hell."

The natural instinct (and mine, until I fought it) is to have as little communication with the imminent intruder as possible and to pray for a miracle. After all, you certainly don't want to encourage something you don't want, right? Wrong.

The Solution

Once it sinks in that the dreaded deed is inevitable and there is no escape without damaging the relationship, don't drag your heels. Rather, go full speed ahead *toward* the disaster.

I raced into action. The first task in making Nina think I was eager for her visit was to call to ask if she had bought the tickets yet. I sensed she suspected my sincerity because she he hadn't. I chided her, "Nina, do it now because airline fares go sky-high the nearer you get to the holiday." She was pleased with my concern.

My second ploy was spending half an hour online finding her a good cheap flight to buy. When I called to tell her, I heard her distrust dissipating.

I e-mailed her the websites of Sarasota attractions and photos of my favorite beaches. Knowing she was a mall-crawl kind of gal, I listed the shopping centers. That "proved" how much I was looking forward to seeing her. I had convinced Nina that I was as ecstatic about her trip as she. And what had it cost me? Less than one hour total, a small price to pay to make her feel welcome—and me less like a liar and hypocrite.

Here is the payoff for you. If you express extreme enthusiasm *before* an unwanted situation, it deters people from noticing the lack of it during. Therefore, I could drop Nina off at the beach and go about my business, guilt-free, not fearing that she would detect my "emotional leakage" that I wanted some time away from her.

This Little Trick is not just for unwanted guests. It helps you handle practically all situations where you want to conceal your lack of enthusiasm. It camouflages negativity about unwanted projects at work, trips and visits you must make, events you are obliged to attend, clients you must entertain, and a variety of other bummers.

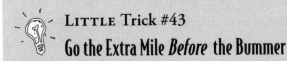

LITTLE Trick #43
Go the Extra Mile *Before* the Bummer

When you are trapped like a bug in a bottle with no escape, don't just accept it. Race toward it with gusto. Find excuses to contact the people involved several times beforehand with zeal. It blinds them to your negativity, and you don't need to be nervously on guard every minute you're with them.

So far in this part, we've talked about getting someone to accept your invitation and how to turn down others' invitations. We've also handled what to do when you're just plain stuck and can't get out of one. Now let's address an all-too-common mistake that makes people wish they'd never invited you—and ensures they will never invite you again.

How to Prevent People Wishing They'd Never Invited You

If your life were a movie, you would have stars, a supporting cast, and extra characters. Single people are constantly "auditioning" their dates to find a "costar," a hero or heroine to live with happily ever after.

Some years ago, I met a man whom I thought might be mine. Gordon was good looking, a fabulous conversationalist, somewhat successful, and, I thought, intelligent. He owned a small travel agency that catered to only "the rich and famous." He was perfect for the role.

I ran into Gordon at several parties and hoped he would ask me out. Sadly, he did not. So I searched for a smooth way to get together. Finally, the perfect opportunity presented itself.

A company was considering me for a consulting assignment to help with their internal communications. The CEO, Milt Feinstein, and director of marketing, Deborah Jordon, had asked me to join them for dinner at an upscale restaurant. Since they were including their spouses, they invited me to bring a date. Seconds after they called, I was on the phone to Gordon.

The big night arrived. During cocktails, we chatted comfortably. Gordon was a real charmer. The evening was off to a great start.

Trouble Begins

When the waiter came, everyone gave their order promptly so they could get on with the conversation. But Gordon had been studying the menu as though preparing for the bar exam. He asked the waiter for a full description of the lobster stuffed with asparagus and the spicy tuna tartar with grilled-quail salad. The rest of the table waited patiently while the waiter described the sautéing, the grilling, and even the provenance of the lobster.

Milt and Deborah looked at each other. I looked down at my lap.

Don't be a meathead, Gordon. These people are here to discuss important business—and you are taking ten minutes to assure your stomach is satisfied.

Not being content with the waiter's description, Gordon said, somewhat rudely, "Oh, just bring me the lobster." Which, not so incidentally, was the most expensive dish on the menu.

After Gordon's stomach show was over, our conversation returned to company business. The two invited spouses understood the reason for the evening; quite appropriately, neither of them interjected opinions into the corporate conversation.

But not Gordon. Everyone was taken aback when he changed the subject to topics of more interest to him.

Shut your mouth, Gordon! They want to talk about something that that is crucial to their company. Don't you get it? I have a stake in the corporate conversation, too, since they are considering me as a consultant.

Thus, Gordon lost his "hero" role in my life, and I recast him to a supporting role. I managed to get the discussion back to the agenda of the evening by asking about the company's perception of their communication needs. But when Gordon jumped in with his own small company's communication challenges, I realized this character would never play *any* role in my life. Sadly, the company didn't, either. Thanks a lot, Gordon.

It Happens Every Day

It's not just social invitations where people misunderstand their temporary roles. The taxi driver talks too much about himself, the housekeeper takes personal calls, the partying executive gives unrequested advice. They are all extras in your life *at that particular moment.* In other situations, the roles are reversed. The waiter, the housekeeper, or the executive is the star, and you are nothing but an extra in their lives. Don't make it about you when it is not about you.

Except for 100-percent-certified purely social gatherings, there is usually a reason for a get-together. Look at the big picture and figure out whether you should be up front or in the background. When conversation turns to the raison d'être, unless you are relevant to it, smile—with sealed lips.

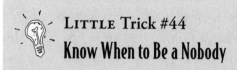

LITTLE Trick #44
Know When to Be a Nobody

Whenever you have contact with people, it's a "show" of sorts. If you are germane to the plot, participate. If you are not, don't steal the show. If you try, the other characters will disconnect from you—permanently.

The next Little Trick helps you get the best bang for your buck when you are picking up the tab.

How to Impress Guests

The arrival of the check is a dramatic moment in any restaurant dining experience. You may handle it in a variety of ways, but the most difficult is when both parties want to pay.

You and your friend have just finished your meal. The waiter lays the check on your table. Boom! To an earsplitting duet of "Let me get that," you and your friend's hands swoop down on it like two pelicans plunging for the same fish. Embarrassing battles ensue. You disturb nearby diners. You embarrass the waiter. And you both sound tacky and money obsessed.

Here's how to avoid this travesty. Arrive at the restaurant before your guest arrives, and give the person who seats you your credit card. Say you want him to bring the bill with the credit card already stamped as you finish your meal because you don't want your friend fighting for it.

When the meal is over, the server brings the check directly to you. You merely fill in the tip and hand it back. When your friend or colleague starts with the "Oh no" bit, simply say "No, it's done. I really want to get this one." Friend is impressed and pleased.

A Tip for Smart Single Women

If you have been dating a gentleman for a while and feel it is your turn, do not *obviously* pay the check at the end. The average male would rather die than have someone at an adjoining table see him give in.

Ladies, arrive at the restaurant early and give your credit card as above. Your date may protest at the end, but secretly he's thinking . . .

She rocks!

Little Trick #45 is not just for restaurants. It works beautifully for movies, sporting events, concerts, clubs, watering holes that have a cover charge—or anywhere else that filthy lucre must change hands ahead of time.

When You Want to Look like a High Roller

Now let's take a giant step up the human food chain to the very exclusive French restaurant Le Posh. White table cloths, tuxedoed waiters, outlandishly expensive, first class all the way.

You are entertaining some VIPs or perhaps a special person you are pursuing, and you want to make a first-class impression.

Right after the appetizers, excuse yourself to "to go to the restroom." Instead, find the maître d' and surreptitiously hand him your credit card saying, "Please make an imprint of this, add an 18 percent gratuity, and I'll sign it now." When you shake his hand (with at least a ten-dollar bill in yours), remind him of your name. That way, he will be sure to use it when he comes to your table at the end of your dinner to tell the group, "It's all taken care of."

Now, you have two choices for this grand finale.

1. The maître d' brings only your presigned receipt. You have impressed your party that you must be a regular at Le Posh and have a house account.
2. If you trust the establishment, tell the maître d' to bring nothing (just his big ingratiating smile) to bid you and your party adieu. This time clients are awed, assuming Le Posh is so honored you are dining there that it is "on the house."

Little Trick #45
Impress Your Friends with a Prepaid Treat

When you want to pick up the tab with a friend, get to the restaurant or event and prepay. That obviates any argument and confirms that you are pretty cool.

When it's important to impress your guest(s) to the max, add a few steps like signing the bill sight unseen, filling in the server's tip ahead of time, and crossing the palm of the obsequious maître d' with some green. The higher the tip, the deeper his fawning will be at the end.

Then all you have to do is enjoy the overwhelmed expressions of your soon-to-be-regular clients or girlfriend.

PART SIX

THIRTEEN LITTLE TRICKS

to Be a Cool Communicator

How to Play It Cool When You're Late

Mr. Cohn, the CEO of an insurance company I consulted for, called a meeting with the entire staff. Everyone had assembled, but it was quite apparent that Sandra, an excellent claims adjustor whom he had just hired, had not arrived. He was obviously disappointed because, in the short time Sandra was working there, she had won his highest respect.

Mr. Cohn started the meeting anyway. About ten minutes into the summit, a tardy Sandra walked in at a normal pace and simply said, "Excuse me," to the group. She took her seat with complete composure.

I could tell from her colleagues' faces that they were thinking, "Well, what's *her* excuse?" The meeting progressed, and Sandra participated with as much self-assurance as though she had been the first to arrive.

Another ten minutes into the meeting, Sandra had a question. She prefaced it by saying, "Perhaps this was answered at the beginning of the meeting, but I may have missed it. My son woke up this morning with a temperature of one hundred and three, and I had to wait until my sister arrived to take him to the doctor." She then continued with her question without a pause.

It was suddenly evident from everyone's face that they felt not only sympathy for her, but increased respect. Why? Because Sandra hadn't slunk in with a mortified expression blurting out her excuse.

After the meeting, several supportive colleagues—including Mr. Cohn—went to her office to ask how her son was. Sandra's dauntless manner of disclosing her tardiness impressed everyone.

Of course she couldn't leave her sick son alone to come to the office, and her not being overly apologetic indicated that she was decisive. She was accustomed to making decisions and not vacillating about them. Perhaps more importantly Sandra's lack of an immediate excuse made it obvious that the others didn't intimidate her, even though she was "the new kid on the block."

Showing confidence in your choices and not being overly anxious about what others think of you are two critical big cat qualities in business. So is knowing when and when not to say, "I'm sorry." Men often argue that mouthing those two little words are admission of guilt. Women usually contend it is merely a gracious way to handle a situation. Bottom line—be aware of which gender you are dealing with in any situation.

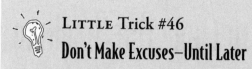

Little Trick #46
Don't Make Excuses—Until Later

Do not demean yourself with an immediate excuse. When you are late to a meeting or anything else, don't slink in like a panting dog brandishing an excuse between his teeth. A gracious "excuse me" suffices.

Later in the proceedings, find an unflustered way to allude honestly to the terrible traffic, the delayed dentist, the afflicted animal, or your feverish five-year-old. When you use this Little Trick, you come across as secure and sincere, not obsessed with other people's opinions of you.

The only downside to this Little Trick is you can't use it too often. If you are habitually late, turn the page and pretend you never read this chapter.

Now, here is a sweet Little Trick to use if you're ever guilty of a much bigger crime than being late!

How to Come Out Smelling like a Rose When You're as Guilty as Heck

As kids, we all had favorite comic book characters. I kept mine a secret because I thought it wasn't normal for a little girl to like a tough character like Wonder Woman. The cartoonist described her as having "the Speed of Hermes, the Wisdom of Athena, the strength of Hercules, and the beauty of Aphrodite." And I just *loved* her hot thigh-high red boots.

My favorite part was when she deflected laser beams with her supercool silver bracelets. "Zap!" "Pow!" "Ping!" Her arms spun around faster than the speeding bullets shooting straight at her. She was confident, yet calm. My Wonder Woman was invincible.

Little Trick #47 will make you invincible to people's piercing verbal shots. I learned it from a female politician who fended off a potentially lethal verbal bullet in a televised news conference.

There was an extremely grave situation in the United States at the time. Many blamed it on the president, who made a quick—and soon unpopular—decision on how to handle it.

Wonder Woman's Pow Pings!

Partway through the news conference, an enraged journalist accused, "Even though some of your fellow Democrats voted against it, weren't you convinced it was the right course of action, and didn't you cast your vote in favor of it?"

Most of us earthlings would have responded with a cautious little "yes," quickly followed by a big loud "BUT . . ." Not this Wonder Woman. She handled it with the "speed of Hermes and the wisdom of Athena."

She looked him right in the eyes, smiled, and said, "You have asked an excellent question, and I'm glad you brought that up." The crowd gasped almost audibly at her reaction. "Yes, you are right. I was convinced it was the right course of action, and I did cast my vote for it." Now the crowd was stunned—and impressed by her candor.

Did you notice the progression of her strategy?

1. She first praised the journalist, thus feeding his ego and deflating his accusatory demeanor.
2. By saying, "I'm glad you brought that up," she craftily convinced the crowd that the question did not cow her. In fact, she implied, she welcomed it.
3. Then she really blew them away. She repeated the journalist's accusations *verbatim*. "Yes, you are right. I was convinced that it was the right course of action, and I did cast my vote for it."

Wonder Woman paused for this to sink in with the crowd. Only then did she proceed to the fourth step and clarify her reasoning. When finished, she said "Thank you, Mr. (journalist's name) for giving me the opportunity to explain this."

It was a knockout. She had obviously won this round.

You Too Can Be Invincible in Four Easy Steps

The next time someone accuses you of something, and you are, indeed guilty, use the politician's "Come Out Smelling like a Rose" Little Trick.

First, throw your accuser off guard by telling her you are happy she brought it up. Secondly, repeat her *precise* words. If she accuses you of "stealing" it, do not change that to "took." If she charges you with "covering up the truth," don't tweak it to "I didn't tell you." In addition, never use the words *but* or *however* after your courageous admission. That is a signal that an excuse is coming. If you committed the act, face it—no weasel words.

The next crucial step is to pause a few seconds. Then continue with a confident-sounding explanation of your reason, the misunderstanding, the mix-up, the confusion, the whatever. But do not make it sound like an excuse.

If there is no justification for your dirty deed, tell them what you learned from it. It works beautifully. Try it!

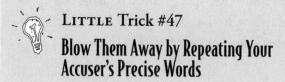

Blow Them Away by Repeating Your Accuser's Precise Words

Here is the game plan when you are guilty. Dead wrong. Caught red-handed.

1. Listen calmly until your accuser finishes, and then say, "I am happy you brought that up."
2. Proceed by saying, "You are right," and repeat his accusation *word for word*. No ifs, ands, or buts—and no changing his precise words.
3. Pause.
4. Then, and only then, with no defensiveness, tell your reasoning. If there is absolutely no rationalization for what you did, tell him what you have learned from it.

To add frosting to the cake, thank your accuser for the opportunity to tell him. It floors him—which is the proper position for him to kiss your hot red boots.

You're Never Too Young to Be Smart

Parents, imagine sitting at the dinner table with your family. Dad, you sternly look at your ten-year-old and state accusatorily, "Mom told me you stood on a chair in the kitchen today and stole some Oreo cookies out of the cookie jar."

Your kid calmly says, "I'm glad you brought that up, Dad. Mom is absolutely right. I stood on a chair in the kitchen today and stole some Oreo cookies out of the cookie jar."

Pause.

"A kid took my lunch box today, and I hadn't eaten anything since this morning. I will be more careful in the future and put my lunch box in a safe place. Thanks for letting me explain that, Dad."

You gotta love the kid, no matter what he says after that.

# How to Come Across as Dependable and Competent

Have you ever wanted to shoot a customer service rep to get revenge? I have. At the last minute, though, I realized revenge wouldn't feel as sweet in an eight-by-ten cell.

After an exhausting plane ride, I staggered into a car rental agency in Kansas City, where I was giving a seminar. The next day I had to drive to Wichita for another. The agent informed me there were no midsize cars, but I could have a subcompact. Not wanting to risk my life dodging motorcycles and Mack trucks, I asked if he'd have a larger car tomorrow.

"Sure," he confidently assured me. "I'll give you the sub-compact today and have a midsize for you tomorrow."

"Well, OK," I mumbled, looking at his name tag. "Are you sure, Samir? I must leave at five."

"No problem," he smiled.

I couldn't take the chance he was wrong, so I asked if he would leave a message for me at the hotel.

"Sure." Same smile.

"I'm staying at the Hyatt Regency," I said, "and the number is 816-123-1234."

"Sure, I'll call you as soon as it comes in."

"Uh, aren't you going to write it down?" I asked.

"Nope, I got it."

"In a pig's eye," I muttered as I left. I floored the gas pedal on the subcompact and left rubber on the road.

While riding the elevator to my hotel room, I knew there was a snow cone's chance in a sauna that I'd hear from Samir. So I called him from my cell to remind him of his promise and my number.

Another man answered at the rental agency. I spit out my story and concern about the subcompact.

"Not to worry, Ms. Lowndes, Samir already left a message for you on your room extension. We are saving both a midsize and a full-size for you in case you change your mind. Just let me know, and we will have it delivered to the Hyatt Regency, front entrance, at five."

"Oh . . . well, uh, gee that's great. Thanks very much."

He must have sensed my lingering suspicion. "And, not to worry about Samir," he said. "He's one of my best employees. Never forgets a thing."

As I hung up, did I credit Samir for his competence? No way! Right Brain was asking my left, "Well, why the heck didn't he write it down?"

"Schmuck," Left Brain said, "Samir is smart, and he didn't need to."

"Yes he did!" Right Brain shouted back. "He may know he'll remember. But I'm the customer. It's his job to make the customer know he'll remember."

"Well, I guess you are correct, Right Brain. I apologize."

It's Perfect for the Office

Obviously, writing directions is not just to comfort cynical customers. Whenever people are giving you even slightly complicated instructions, write them down to set their hearts at rest. Can you imagine how impressed your supervisor would be as you listen to her intently and then make little hen scratchings on your notepad? You could have the memory of an elephant and be as dependable as your next heartbeat, but if you don't write it down, she might doubt that you really "got it."

And for Friends, Too

Taking notes also works when dealing with pals—especially those unemotional, organized types like my platonic male roommate. Phil is kind, even tempered, and extremely organized, not my strong suits. His pen, notepad, scotch tape, and stapler reside in precisely the same spot next to his computer on his desk all year long. If I borrow the pen and put it back on the wrong side of his desk, he doesn't even look for it. He just asks if I've seen it. However, his tight smile reveals intense aggravation.

When it finally dawned on me that Phil was the thinker/perfectionist type, I decided to try something. During our next conversation, I kept a pad nearby and occasionally scrawled on it anything I should remember.

Phil's reaction was incredible! I saw his respect-o-meter shoot straight up through the skylight. Now I keep a pad and pencil handy whenever he and I are going to discuss something. And he no longer considers me desperately disorganized.

Little Trick #48
Write It Down, Even if You Don't Need To

Even though you know you "got it," let others know you do with pen and paper in hand. While writing, don't forget to look up at them occasionally with those insightful "I understand everything" eyes—then dive back into your notes. It is an insurance policy that they will sleep better at night and be awed by your competence.

The next Little Trick is not so much to impress people as it is to make them think you are impressed by them.

How to Talk Behind People's Backs so They Love It

For a few years, I was a flight attendant. Tova Svensson was the most popular flight attendant I flew with, and we shared many experiences over the years. She and I went to refresher trainings at the airport together, ran into flight crews around the terminal, and occasionally double-dated on layovers.

The one thing that puzzled me about this poised Swedish flight attendant was that occasionally she would speak a few sentences in a much louder voice. Then her volume would go back to normal. It seemed strange, so I decided to monitor it.

The next time she said something rather loudly, we were leaving a training class at the hangar. As we went through the door, she said, "Ya, that instructor is really good. I got a lot out of the class." Of course, the instructor overheard it.

Tova Strikes Again

Full-volume comment #2: Walking away from a colleague we had just talked to in the terminal, she said, "She's really nice. Have you ever flown with her?" The other flight attendant couldn't help but overhear it.

Hmm . . .

My suspicions were proven when we went to a party on a layover the following week. On the way out, the host waved goodbye to us from his doorstop. Ten yards away, Tova said loudly, "Ya, that was really a fun party." Naturally, the partygiver heard it.

Very clever Little Trick, Tova! She made it a point to compliment the teacher, the flight attendant, and the partygiver *supposedly* to me—but slightly louder so the person being complimented could hear it. Now I know one reason she was so popular.

LITTLE Trick #49
Let People Overhear Your Compliment

The only thing nicer than hearing a compliment is *over*hearing it. Your parents probably told you, "Don't talk about people behind their back." Let's change that to, "Do talk about people behind their back—if you're saying nice things about them." Just be sure to say it loud enough for them to hear it.

Have you ever had a great conversation with someone but you don't know what she said? In fact, you don't even remember what you were discussing—or even what *you* said. You just know you feel relaxed whenever you're speaking with her.

It just might have something to with the next Little Trick. Try to make it second nature every time you sit down to speak with people.

How to Make Everyone Comfortable Speaking with You

While I was riding my bicycle one Sunday morning, a German shepherd decided to amuse itself by chasing me. Peeling away at full speed, I frantically looked back to see how close he was. I won the race but wound up in a hospital bed with a twisted neck.

That evening, a man I was seeing and a friend of his came to visit me. Scott sat right by my side and his buddy at the foot of the bed. I couldn't turn my head to look at him directly, but my peripheral vision told me Scott looked uncharacteristically annoyed. I figured it was sympathy for me and dismissed it.

Cut to the following Saturday. We were having dinner at a restaurant, and the server delivered her entire dramatic monologue about the specials to Scott. Afterward, I groused, "Well, she could have looked my way at least once."

"C'mon, Leil, you didn't look at me once when you were in the hospital. But you sure couldn't take your eyes off my friend," he said, accusatorially.

"I *couldn't* look at you, Scottie," I said. "You were sitting right beside me. You were a pain in the neck, a physical pain in the neck, to talk to. But your friend was in my direct line of vision. You should have put your chair where I could see you without twisting my neck."

This experience made me exquisitely aware of something we seldom consider. A comfortable conversation involves more than just your words and body language. It includes *where* you and your conversational partners are sitting, and how comfy they are.

When entertaining, most people would ensure that a guest's chair isn't too hard or bright sunlight from a window isn't blinding him. But that's often where it stops. To fully enjoy a conversation with you, people must experience no physical discomfort or stress caused by your relative positions.

For example, if you want a friendly exchange in the office, don't ask someone to sit on the other side of your desk from you. That can be intimidating. Put a chair by the side of your desk instead. If the two of you will be talking in a conference room, let the other person enter first and choose a chair.

If you are half of a couple conversing with someone, don't sit so far apart that she has to swivel her head back and forth like watching a tennis game. Even if you are sitting on a couch with someone side by side, slide your bottom an appropriate distance away so he can turn to look at you without straining his neck.

The next time you are chatting with someone in a wheel-chair, don't stand where she will get a sore neck looking up at you. Sit on her level or stand far enough away so you are comfortably in her line of sight.

Be especially compassionate when conversing with elderly people. Every decade, rotating their heads becomes more difficult for them. Also, they probably don't want to sit on a low couch where getting up is a struggle. When chatting with the seventy-plus set, offer them a higher chair with a straight back—and place it where they can see your lips in case they are hard of hearing.

Think of your relative seating positions like *feng shui*, the ancient Chinese art of arranging furniture and other elements to eliminate discordance. Choose your seat—and theirs—to obtain optimum comfort for all.

After all, if the Chinese do it for their dead, you can do it for your living friends.

LITTLE Trick #50
Assure Your Conversation Partner's Physical Comfort

When you enter someone's home or office, don't just plop down anywhere. Pick your perch with care. When entertaining, offer seats keeping in mind your guests' ages, abilities, status (which we'll discuss later), and their sex. Relative positioning affects the encounter more than you can imagine.

When It Comes to Males, There Is More to Consider!

Sisters, when I was growing up, psychologists, psychiatrists, and feminists tried to convince us that men and women were alike. In the big "nature versus nurture" turmoil, the majority cast their votes on the nurture side.

But in this so-called "century of enlightenment," neurosurgeons have ascertained otherwise. Their finely tuned instruments point to precise clumps of neurons that, while not pink or blue, do indicate gender proclivities. One of those tendencies for a male is that sitting where he can't see the door is disquieting for him at the least, devastating at most.

Perhaps it comes from watching too many cowboy movies. If the gun-slinging dude wearing the white hat didn't face the saloon door, the bad guy in the black hat could blast him in the back. Whatever the origin, sharp people today are savvy about the gender seat game and play it skillfully.

Ladies, let's say you walk into a restaurant and have chosen a table. Be sure to leave the "best seat" for him. The best seat, in his estimation, is not the one with the nicest view, nor the warmest in winter or the coolest in summer. If you want a happy puppy at your table, give him the one facing the door.

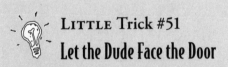 LITTLE Trick #51

Let the Dude Face the Door

They haven't isolated the specific gene that makes men jumpy sitting with their backs to the door. But trust the inexplicable, indisputable truth.

Sisters, upon entering the restaurant, the meeting, the whatever, go for the seat that puts *your* back to the door. Our neurons can take it. Theirs can't.

Wait, It Gets More Complicated

While the following tips are generalizations, of course, put your tongue in your cheek and keep your eyes open to see who wants whom to sit where.

Ladies, would you believe that where a man invites you to sit can reveal how he feels about you? And gentlemen, did you know that the chair she instinctively chooses indicates her sentiments about you?

You probably know that sitting across from one other creates a distance. Ladies, sitting or being invited to sit on his left signifies, "Let's be friends, but nothing more."

Sitting on his right hints the opposite. Why? Because a man always wants "his" woman on his right. I know, I don't get it either. It's a guy thing.

Gentlemen, It Gets Competitive

Fellows, the facing-the-door dilemma is trickier for you because, to make your male colleague, friend, or boss more relaxed, you must turn your testosterone meter down and overcome uneasiness to sit with your back to the door. (Shudder.)

We women will never understand it. When it's purely social, girlfriends seldom care where they sit—unless there is a desirable male in the room.

The art and science of tush placement is entirely different in the social arena and the business world. Let's now travel from pleasure to business.

How to Make People Look Up to You

How many times have you hemmed and hawed about which seat to choose on a plane? A window seat? An aisle seat? The front of the plane or the back? For a short ride, does it really matter much?

Other places we sit, however, do matter. Where you put your glutes in negotiations or certain corporate situations is a lot more significant than where you sit above the clouds.

The first rule is to stake out your seat strategically if it is going to be an ongoing situation. Changing your chair later can cause corporate or social civil war.

Last May, I was giving an all-day seminar for a contact lens company on the subject of change. As is usual with a large program, participants sit wherever they like as they enter.

All morning, we discussed the importance of flexibility in today's corporate environment. Everyone agreed employees' openness to change was crucial to the success of a company.

Just before lunch, I took half the participants, Group A, to a smaller training room. I quietly asked them, "Don't mention this to the rest of the participants, but please return ten minutes early after lunch—and sit in a different chair from where you sat this morning."

After Lunch

At 1:20, most of the Group A participants had returned and were snuggled into different seats. At 1:30, when Group B started ambling in, I heard a gentle medley of "Uh, excuse me, I think you're sitting in my seat," and "Sorry, this seat is occupied." Gradually, the volume rose, becoming a cacophony of "What's the matter?" "You can't find another chair?"

Then near pandemonium ensued. "You are sitting in the wrong chair." "That is *my* seat!" Some of the shyer participants stood at the door in shock. Others, protesting under their breath, found new seats but were still stunned that someone had "stolen" theirs. A few diehards continued trying to dislodge the occupant who had usurped their rightful roost.

Before long, a few unseated participants started giggling. They caught on that the whole thing was an exercise showing how people resist change. Finally, everybody got it and had a big laugh.

Here is what was really huge, however. After the exercise was over, the seat-stealers stood up and returned to their original morning perches!

So much for my seminar on change.

Why am I telling you this? Because everything I am about to divulge on power seating is superseded by the fact that people think their original choice of chair is chiseled into stone. So, when entering a room where people traditionally sit in the same seat, don't mess!

Keeping this in mind, let us proceed.

Stay on the Right Side of the Big Shot

Whether spoken or not, there is a boss, leader, or most respected person in almost every gathering. Naturally, he will sit in the catbird seat. To subliminally boost your status with the group, arrive early to assess the seating situation. Figure out where Big Kahuna will probably place his prestigious tush.

Warning! Do not take Papa Bear's seat. You could be sitting on a powder keg.

Do, however, choose the chair directly to his right. This hints you are the head honcho's trusted advisor, or "right-hand person." This "right of the leader" position is so crucial that clever negotiators will arrive at the meeting room early and figure where the opposition leader will sit. Then they put one of *their* negotiators in that right-hand seat—therefore denying the opposition honcho a right-hand person. Dirty pool? Not to negotiators.

LITTLE Trick #52

Take the "Success Seat" on the Kingpin's Right

As you enter a room, situate your soon-to-be-slightly-more-respected tush on the big enchilada's right. To further increase people's perception that you are vital to the VIP, occasionally lean toward him and whisper something in his ear. A hushed "Could you pass the water pitcher, please?" works quite well.

You need not limit Little Trick #52 to professional situations. Sitting directly to the right of the host, honored guest, or most admired person at a dinner party also holds unspoken status.

Another Seating Strategy

Consider the elevation. The higher you sit, the more stature you have. If all the chairs are the same height, look for a desk in the room you can half-sit on. Or is there a couch where you can perch on the arm? Try to find anyplace where others must physically look up to you when you are speaking.

If there is no one sitting place higher than the others, say at a boardroom table, here is a technique that a top negotiator taught me. Jimmi, the best bargainer I ever met, was short in stature but tall in talent—and in trickery. I had been consulting with his company for several months. One time, he and I were the last ones to leave the boardroom after a negotiation. I noticed a small square cushion on his seat. He saw me looking at it and, putting his hands up like a caught criminal, said, "OK, OK, I'll confess. You probably know the reason I have the pillow on the chair."

I took a stab at it. "To make you higher?"

"Right, Leil. But here's something you probably didn't notice." He swiveled his chair and showed me he'd rotated it to full height. He then whispered that he'd swiveled the other side's chairs down. "It puts the opposition at a disadvantage," he winked.

I didn't know whether to be impressed or shocked by his Little Trick. "Well, you did look pretty imposing at the meeting," I murmured.

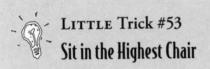

LITTLE Trick #53
Sit in the Highest Chair

Sitting in an elevated seat generates subconscious respect for you and your ideas. Arrive at meetings early and scan the room. Find a throne or build your own.

The same goes for casual social gatherings. Choose the highest seat in the living room. Half-sitting on a couch arm works well in short discussions.

When people have to physically look up to see you, it carries over into psychologically looking up to you. If you must choose between sitting to the right of the host or in the highest chair, go for the latter.

The next chapter explains how to play the height card when standing.

How to Exude a More Authoritative Air

In the Introduction, we discussed how people crave acceptance from those they respect, whereas it has less value from those they don't. By demonstrating authority around your friends, colleagues, and loved ones, you build your muscles to help lift them later.

Jimmi, the big cat who was only five-foot-six, taught me another priceless little practice for gaining prestige. He said, "Leil, show me what you do when you agree with someone." His question perplexed me, but I nodded as usual by lowering my chin several times.

"Isn't that what everybody does?" I asked him.

"No," he whispered as though he were sharing state secrets. "Here's how I do it." He then proceeded to lift his chin up from parallel to the floor, not down. I must admit, it did look more impressive than the usual nod.

Be wary when using this Little Trick because, if the rest of your body language is not friendly, you could come off as arrogant. However, if you blend this confident move with other warm gestures, people will appreciate such an authoritative-looking person—you—agreeing with them.

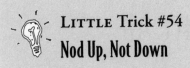

Little Trick #54
Nod Up, Not Down

Begin with your chin parallel to the floor. Then, to express acceptance or agreement, lift your chin up and bring it back to normal several times. This way, you are conveying confidence. Jimmi calls a bowed head the "Beat me again, master" position—don't send that message!

Women, I especially urge you to use this Little Trick for more reasons than just looking self-assured. Since a man is usually taller, you keep better eye contact with him while nodding up. And if you dye your hair, why show him the roots?

The next Little Trick is for exuding an air of authority in your written communication.

How to Make Your Signature 21 Percent More Prestigious

I am sure it comes as no surprise to you that direct marketing folks and professional fund-raisers lie awake at night planning how to squeeze money out of a stone.

Please don't misunderstand me. I am not talking about the legions of altruistic men and women who volunteer their valuable time raising funds for worthy causes. Nor about those who ask for contributions to our grossly underfunded cultural institutions.

I'm talking about direct mail (DM) pros, the ones who know how to shoot a million sitting ducks with one hot DM letter. They conjure up schemes to make people dash for their checkbooks, credit cards, and cash-stashed cookie jars.

Some DM letters tell you that you, too, can be the "proud new owner" of whatever overpriced doohickey they're hawking that month. Other letters yank at your heartstrings so you will send money to feed starving crippled children in Chonesia (a country that doesn't exist.) DM professionals go to expensive seminars to learn what "suckers," ahem, I mean, "letter recipients," respond to.

I will share a simple technique that they all swear by—but only if you promise not to use it to inveigle little old ladies into sending you their life savings for mutilated children in Montepenia or to sell overpriced junk that breaks a week later.

Other than that, you may employ this Little Trick to make all your written communications look more prestigious and trustworthy.

A study published in the *Journal of Social Psychology* established that a handwritten signature in *blue* ink is 21 percent more effective than one in black ink. And in direct marketing, that is *huge*!

The next time you get a DM letter from some of the biggies like *Publishers Clearinghouse*, you will see the text is black, but the signature is blue. Direct marketing mavens know that this is so important that they go to the incredible expense of a two-color print job—just for the blue signature. And just think that you can do it free!

LITTLE Trick #55
Sign Everything in Blue Ink

Your sky blue signature in a sea of black type stands out as more credible and prestigious than a similar one in black. Splurge for a blue ballpoint pen. It will be the best sixty-nine-cent investment you make in your career.

The next chapter reveals an effective, yet seldom used technique to earn affection and loyalty from those who are not as high on the totem pole as you. I learned it from a manager, but you don't need to be a boss to benefit from it.

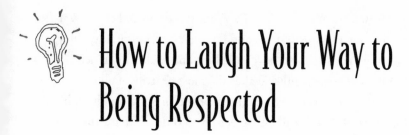

How to Laugh Your Way to Being Respected

Walter is not the most experienced manager I've met. Nor the most trained. He's not the most corporate-looking manager I worked with. Nor is he the most educated. He's not even the handsomest! When I showed him this, he laughed heartily and agreed it's all true.

Most managers, at one time or another, ponder: "Is it better to be liked or respected?" Walter has never had to ask himself that question. He is both. There is no attitude in his department, no grumbling, no gossip nor backstabbing. So what is Walter's magic? What makes his department function so smoothly?

Monday Morning

To find out, I asked Walter to let me sit in on one of their monthly meetings.

8:55 A.M.: As I enter the conference room, everyone is gabbing away about what they did that weekend. But Walter is nowhere in sight.

9:10 A.M.: Walter enters. Everyone stands up and claps. Walter lets out a big belly laugh and says mock accusatorially, "Hey, one of you guys should have called me and said, 'Get in here, ya bum!'" Everyone laughs, Walter the most heartily of all.

"So," he continues tapping a bottle of soda on the table like a gavel. "Let's call this meeting to order. What's the first order of business?"

Steve, his assistant, says, "I don't know." Once again, Walter gives his big belly laugh and everyone joins in. "No, seriously," Steve says, and he proceeds to present a thorough team productivity report on the past week. On Steve's imitation of Daffy Duck's "Th-th-that's all, folks," Walter smiles broadly and claps. Steve takes a deep dramatic bow. Once again, Walter's big belly laugh resounds through the room, and the rest of the team joins in.

Are you beginning to get the picture? Walter's employees feel clever, competent, connected, and appreciated by their boss. He seems to thoroughly enjoy their sometimes pretty lame humor. His big laugh is contagious, and his team actually looks forward to their weekly meetings. Every one of Walter's employees would go the extra mile for him.

Have I told you enough so you can answer the question of the day: "What was Walter's secret weapon?" You got it. It was his big jovial laugh that one and all loved hearing.

This is not to say that *everyone* should use laughter in business. While it makes the workplace pleasanter, perpetual laughter, or even one laugh at the wrong time, could reduce you to little puss status. Guffawing too much might make people think you're a goof-off. And laughing at a superior's jokes might make others think you are brown-nosing.

The point of this chapter is that if you are *above* someone in hierarchy, your warm laugh makes her feel comfortable with you and confident of her own abilities—qualities that everyone needs to do a good job. Walter obviously understood this about his team.

When you're on the top of the heap, laughter can be a powerful discipline device, too. Read on.

If an Employee Messes Up

Now, lest you think our Walter was a Walter Mitty pushover, let me tell you about another weapon Walter wielded. It is a razor-sharp technique that, happily, he seldom had to use on an employee. Simply *withholding* his humor and giving the staffer a stern look was enough to let the employee know that he isn't pleased. Coming from a regular, straight-faced boss, this look would have made the employee defensive. That could lead to attitude, complaints, gossip, backstabbing, and all the other omnipresent morale killers.

Walter never raised his voice or expressed irritation. An icy look was enough to get his employees back on track. They felt remorse, not resentment, that they had let their friend down.

I have observed Walter in other meetings with his fellow managers and superiors. He is somewhat serious when interacting with them and doesn't laugh much. Seeing him in action with his team made me realize that his big laugh was a conscious choice and, for him, an extremely effective management tool.

Is this to say laughter is the next big fad following on the heels of Reengineering, Empowerment, TQM, and climbing up poles with your colleagues in the name of team building?

Of course not. It is simply the story of how one manager got the best out of his people by using laughter as his magic wand.

You may not be a boss in the corporate sense, but you are, no doubt, more advantaged than dozens of others in your life. Do you have a less fortunate friend? A timid colleague? A sick or elderly neighbor? A younger sibling who looks up to you? Contemplate the incredible power that a colossal laugh at their (sometimes weak) humor has to lift their life.

Little Trick #56
Connect with a "Lesser" Through Laughter

When you are Top Dog in any situation, laughter works wonders with your "underling(s)." It doesn't make someone do something for you, it makes her *want* to—and that is a hundred times more powerful. Laugh a lot in appreciation of those lower on the social or business totem pole. You not only please them, you build their loyalty.

Now to a somewhat opposite situation. Say you don't want to draw certain people closer. In fact, you want as much distance from them as possible—but to still retain their respect and affection. Tough task! However, Little Trick #57 accomplishes just that.

 # How to Escape Bores Without Hurting Their Feelings

See if the following scene is familiar to you: It is ten o'clock on a glorious Saturday morning. Cool and crisp, seventy degrees, zero humidity, and a cloudless robin's-egg blue sky. An occasional gust of wind rustles the leaves and tingles your skin, but, within seconds, the warm sun's rays bake it away. As you stroll along the street, you're humming U2's "It's a beautiful day . . . don't let it get away."

Then BLAM! you spot a nascent disaster—that *bore* who always talks your ear off. He can compress the most words into the smallest idea of any man you know. He is the last person on earth you'd want to squander one second of this heavenly day on. But, alas, he has spotted you. It's too late.

"Hey, how ya doin'?" he waves.

"Pretty-good-nice-to-see-you," you speed-say as you pick up your pace and pass him.

"Where didja go on vacation?" he calls back.

Darn, you must now turn back and chat for a bit. At this point, most people's bodies belie their mock friendly words. Like a horse backing away from a cruel handler, they prance backward. Their bucking is obvious and their snorts almost

185

audible. Then they gallop off, leaving their acquaintance feeling like trodden hay.

Do *not* do that to people! Don't ruthlessly perform the rude breakaway dance. Just because you're still facing them, you think they don't notice you are backing away? It's as obvious as thumbing your nose at them.

Instead, use the following Little Trick, which speeds you toward salvation and your destination. It also makes the bore admire you more. Sound impossible?

Here's the Plan

When you spot the windbag who wants to snare you into conversation, pick up your speed so he will see you walking briskly as though you are late somewhere. (Your brisk walk confirms your story later.)

When almost within speaking distance to your "friend," feign happy surprise and come to a screeching halt. Greet him enthusiastically.

Do NOT look rushed.

Do NOT step back.

Do NOT start prancing in place.

Train your face to say, "I'm really looking forward to yakking it up with you." Confirm this with an "I've got all the time in the world for you" demeanor. Then DO yak it up—for forty-five seconds. That is the minimum time to qualify it as a bona fide conversation. Look laid back and go nice and slow during your convivial chat.

Then—and only then—look at your watch. Appear disappointed and explain, regretfully, you are late for a meeting, a date, an appointment, a funeral, a whatever.

Now, here is the most important move. Walk away at a leisurely pace but, when you get about ten feet from him, break into a canter. Race away as though you were making up for the time you lost because you really preferred to stay and chat.

He's thinking to himself . . .

Whatta guy! He was really rushed. But he wanted to talk to me so much that he risked being late.

This screeching to a halt, microchatting, then racing away like hell Little Trick is also effective in the corporate halls of our great work-obsessed country. Not only does it get you away from the office bore you encounter in the hall, it makes you look like you are rushing to get your work done, too!

LITTLE Trick #57
Walk Away Slowly, Then Let Them See You Sprint

A quick review on how to escape a bore in five easy steps.

1. Wave enthusiastically when you first spot her.
2. Stop and chat, unrushed, for forty-five seconds.
3. Look at your watch and act disappointed.
4. Walk slowly away.
5. After a few yards, break into a sprint and run like hell.

Now she feels valued, you retain her respect, and it didn't take any longer than the insulting white rabbit break dance.

How to Read People's Minds

About six months ago, I was insecure about a chapter I had written for this book, so I asked a good friend, Ann Torrago, to read it. Ann is a warmhearted person so, even if the chapter made her gag, she would never tell me.

I gave her the manuscript and strategically sat in another chair across the room. While I pretended to read the newspaper, I was furtively peering over the paper at Ann's face. Her deadpan expression confirmed my suspicion. In spite of her later compliments, I knew my chapter was the pits.

A few weeks later, I was telling the Ann story to the son of a friend of mine. Jonathan Rahm is a trainer and talented "horse whisperer" in Suffolk County, New York. A horse whisperer reads horses' feelings by watching their ear positions, tail movements, respiratory rate, nostrils, and other signals that riders with shattered kneecaps obviously missed. When I finished, he said, "Yeah, it's easier to read a person than a horse."

"You've got to be kidding, Jonathan! People can fake their emotions. Horses can't."

He responded, "Sure, Leil, people can fake it when they think they are being watched. But watch them when they think they aren't, when they're off guard. That's when you get the real story. I like to think of it as being a 'people whisperer.'"

This insight by a twenty-six-year-old stunned me with its obvious truth: Lips can lie while speaking. But lips tell the truth when they think no one is looking. I researched the subject and discovered that science is now paying some pretty serious attention to the fleeting, split-second expressions that slip across our faces thousands of times each day. Daniel McNeill, author of *The Face: A Natural History*, wrote, "In the last 20 years, we've learned more about the communicative power of the face than in the previous 20 millennia."

By connecting facial expression to brain activity with extraordinary precision, researchers are discovering that, in a sense, it is possible to "read" someone's mind. And, when you learn to do it too, you become an exquisitely better communicator. Just imagine how much more persuasive and sensitive you'll be when you know what people are thinking!

Let's say you are at an office meeting and your team leader proposes a change in direction for the current project. But you don't agree. Glance at your colleagues' faces. Do they have a microscopic hint of a frown? Or are their lips and eyes softer? If the latter, you know you'll be the lone voice against the change. Therefore, even if you do speak up, you won't be successful.

When watching a DVD with a friend, momentarily take your eyes off the screen and sneak a peek at his face. No mystery there. You can easily determine if your friend is enjoying the film or not.

You can track everyone's emotions pretty accurately from his or her subtle, supposedly unseen, expressions. How subtle?

Well, the next sunny weekend that you're at the beach, watch the sunbathers on sandy towels soaking up the rays. They're not smiling, but if you focus on their mouths, you'll see an ever-so-slight lifting at the corners. Then, while driving to work on Monday morning, glance at other drivers in a traffic jam. Lifted lips are as rare as a solar eclipse.

The difference in facial expressions is more obvious when you have access to both at the same time. At an airport, gaze first at the faces of people waiting for their loved ones to come out the exit. Now compare them with the expressions of limousine drivers holding a sign with their unknown passenger's name on it.

The first expression is not a smile. It is just a minuscule lifting of the muscles on either side of the mouth. The second expression is not a frown. The limousine drivers simply have a deadpan expression.

The Social Benefits

Gentlemen, wouldn't it be nice to know whether your date, who said she likes baseball, is really enjoying the game? If she is straight-faced, don't invite her to another one or you might get turned down—then wonder why. (Incidentally, if she catches you looking at her, don't worry. She'll take it as a compliment.)

Ladies, watch your husband's face while he's driving to dinner at the in-laws. You'll get the story on how he *really* feels about it.

And kids are naturals at face reading. Did you ever see a kid take his eyes off Mom's expression when she's reading his report card?

LITTLE Trick #58
Read their Lips—When They're Not Speaking

Like a pilot scanning the horizon for other planes, make it a habit to scan the faces in any group. Pay special attention to the corners of their lips. When you are able to "read their minds," your Emotional Prediction meter shoots straight up. Therefore, your skill in communicating will almost double. No exaggeration. I promise.

Incidentally, this Little Trick has already benefited you. Why? If it hadn't been for Ann's bored expression, you too would be subjected to that tedious chapter I deleted.

PART SEVEN

TWELVE LITTLE TRICKS

*to Avoid the Thirteen Most Common
Dumb Things You Should* Never
Say or Do

How to Avoid People Thinking You Have No Status at Your Job

When the big boys and big girls are considering whether to invite someone to join them above the glass ceiling, they listen intently for any hint that the candidate is not the big cheese he or she purports to be. They have such finely tuned ears they can hear a snail clear its throat a mile away. If they pick up on one giveaway phrase, it can turn a potential big cat into roadkill.

One time, I was the littlest shot, a lowly author, at an awards ceremony of the Audio Books Publishing Association. Someone must have screwed up the seating plan, because I found myself at a banquet table with seven heavyweights of the most prestigious audio books publishing house. They were listening intently to a man who was seeking a high-level job with them.

The gentleman spoke of his educational degrees and his extensive track record. Most of all, he described his current high-level responsibilities and position. I glanced around the table and could see he was impressing them.

One big cat handed him his business card and said, "Give me a call tomorrow. I look forward to hearing from you."

"Great," said the soon-to-be-squashed critter. "I'll call you tomorrow on my lunch hour." The heavy hitters froze. They glanced at each other with that knowing "this dude is history" look.

With four words, the poor guy proved he was a little puss who would never make it in the front door of Big Deal Audio Publishing House. He signed his professional death warrant when he said, "Great, I'll call you *on my lunch hour*." To instantly connect professionally with the big boys and girls, you must sound as though you are on the same level.

Why?

Anyone perched high on the professional ladder calls her own shots about little things like lunch. No one tells her what she can do and what she can't do. Least of all, what time to have lunch and when to be back in the office.

Of course, practically everyone who works at an office has more or less an hour to eat, and it's usually the same time each day. Instead of saying, "during my lunch hour," however, don't mention the time allotted. "While I'm at lunch" will suffice.

We're talking semantics here, but they are pretty important ones. If Little Puss had just said, "I'll call you about 12:30" instead, he might soon have heard "Welcome aboard."

LITTLE Trick #59
Don't Say "My Lunch Hour"

When you use this phrase (and others like it, such as "during my break"), your listeners figure somebody above you dictates your schedule. Even though most of us do have someone giving us our schedule, why advertise it? Seek to sound self-directed, not dictated to by someone else.

No matter what professional position you hold or how structured your day, you have the liberty to think and speak like the captain of your own ship. Nobody tells captains when and how long they have for lunch.

Here are some more ways to sound like you are the Big Boss, at least of your own life.

How to Avoid Sounding like Someone Else Rules Your Life

Do you remember your high school teacher saying, "Now students, don't use a pronoun without an antecedent?"

Without a what?

Then Miss Peasgood would tap the blackboard and enlighten you. "An antecedent is a word or word phrase that the subject of the sentence refers to." Ahem, make that "to which the subject refers."

Don't worry, I'm not going to get all grammarian on you. Little Trick #60 has nothing to do with sentence structure. What it concerns is your subconscious view of your own status.

Around office water coolers all over the country, you hear people saying things like:

> "*They* prohibit us from surfing the Internet at lunch."
>
> "*They* won't let us wear jeans on casual Fridays."
>
> "*They* don't care whether we can pay our hospital bills or not."

Question: Who is the big-deal anonymous "they" who makes all the decisions and has power over these people's lives?

Naturally, there are bosses and governing bodies we all have to obey. But why make it obvious? Using the anonymous "they" gives your listeners the impression that you feel like a hopeless victim of "the system."

Don't Sound like a Slave

If you must speak of people who have any power over you, at least be specific.

> "*Management* prohibits us from surfing the Internet at lunch."
>
> "*Human Resources* won't let us wear jeans on casual Fridays."
>
> "*The current administration* doesn't care whether we can pay our hospital bills or not."

 LITTLE Trick #60

Don't Sound Like an "Anonymous They" Rules You

Do yourself a professional and personal favor. Whenever you are talking about people who make certain rules you must obey, be specific. It implies you have the whole picture. You are not a clueless servant who allows yourself to be controlled by a mysterious ruling class called "they."

Take It One Step Further

Want to kick your status up a notch? Go for the gold and sound like you are part of the "ruling class" yourself. Put those who must answer to someone else in a specific group (even though you are part of that group). For example:

> "Management prohibits *the staff* from surfing the Internet at lunch."
> "Human Resources won't let *employees* wear jeans on casual Fridays."
> "The current administration doesn't care whether *families* can pay their hospital bills or not."

Of course, we are part of "the employees," "the staff," or "the families." But, by putting the controlled group in the third person, we don't sound like anyone commands *us*. They are only controlling those other folks.

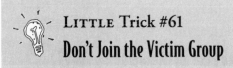 **LITTLE Trick #61**
Don't Join the Victim Group

Disassociate yourself from the crowd somebody else has authority over. Insinuate that nobody controls you. Miss Peasgood says, "Don't start your sentence with the third-person plural pronoun. Also, don't be the object of their domination, singular or plural." Or something like that.

How to Avoid People Saying "Get a Life!"

I will never forget the few fleeting glances two corporate big cats gave each other while interviewing candidates for a job. I was consulting for a start-up insurance company that had hired a number of good people but still needed a crackerjack claims adjuster for one of their new territories. The two executives had scheduled dozens of interviews in the boardroom. They invited me to sit in to throw my impressions into the mix.

By noon, they had spoken to seven candidates. Then the receptionist rang, "A Mr. Kevin Mason arrived early this morning. I know his appointment is at one. But he's been here several hours. Do you think you could squeeze him in before lunch?"

"Uh, sure," Mr. Cohn, the CEO, said. "Send him in." Cohn introduced him to Ms. Engels, the vice president. He added, "I'm sorry you had to wait so long."

"Oh, that's OK," Mason replied. "I came early because I had some time to kill."

ZAP! That was it. The kiss of death. The interview was over. Cohen and Engels rolled their eyes simultaneously as he walked out the door. I was confused until Cohn said, "Right, just what we want. Somebody who kills time."

"Not on *our* time," Engels laughed.

Aha! I got it.

A big cat may have enough prestige to have the direct line to the U.S. president and enough power to silence the toughest critics. Time to vacation? Yes. Time to play? Yes. Time to have loving moments with the family? Of course. Probably even time to party. But what he *doesn't* have is time to kill. If he did, he would never admit it.

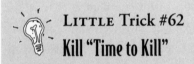

Little Trick #62
Kill "Time to Kill"

The message between those three innocent-sounding words is, "My life is so boring and empty that I can't think of a thing to do with my time. Nothing creative. Nothing productive. Nothing enlightening. Not even anything that would give me or my friends pleasure. What a loser I am."

After a few more disappointing interviews, a striking brunette named Catalina walked in. She had that dynamic corporate look. The two senior executives smiled at each other, stood up, shook her hand, and eagerly scanned her résumé again.

Her answers to all their questions were right on the mark. As they stood up to shake her hand, they said, "You'll be hearing from us." They had found their claims adjuster. Or so they thought until . . .

The candidate smiled and said, "I'm so pleased. And Mr. Cohn, what is your sign?"

"My what?!?"

"Your astrological sign," Catalina said.

"Uh, I'm not really sure," he answered in disbelief. "Well, we appreciate your coming to apply."

The minute she walked out the door, he bunched her résumé into a ball and slam-dunked it into the wastebasket.

Next!

Is it really so horrible that Catalina asked Mr. Cohn's sign? No. He might even be an expert himself in astrology, numerology, and tarot cards and do Reiki healing on the side. He couldn't take the chance, however, that his company's claims adjuster would say something so irrelevant while trying to calm down a client whose car was crushed by a falling tree.

Later that day, another candidate's résumé took a direct flight from Cohn's desk to the shredder because she said "God bless you" as she left the interview.

So what's wrong that? Nothing. It is completely appropriate, lovely in fact, when you are with Christian friends. Muslims say "Peace be with you," and Jews say "Shalom." But one spiritual suit does not fit all. Cohn shuddered imagining his new claims adjuster giving a Christian blessing to a rabbi whose synagogue was whisked away by a tornado.

Until you have further knowledge of someone's faith and passions, stick to the safe stuff. Like "hello" and "good-bye."

So Who Got the Job?

A soon-to-be big cat named Sandra, whom you met in Part Six, was their next candidate. Why did they hire her? Here are just a few reasons.

Sandra's first sentence when walking in for the interview was, "Mr. Cohn and Ms. Engels, I hope for your sake I'm your last interview. You have probably had a grueling day." She had accurately forecast how they would feel at the end of their long day. By commenting on it, she displayed Emotional Prediction—obviously an important trait for a top claims adjuster.

The two executives laughed, "You are *so* right." During the interview, all of Sandra's answers were sensitive and respectful. As the interview neared its close, Sandra casually commented, "Thank you so much for staying late to talk with me. Now I guess you have your real job ahead of you."

Once again, she displayed on-target Emotional Prediction.

Yet Another Smooth Move

Up until now, I had been like a fly on the wall. As Sandra was leaving, she nodded and thanked me briefly, too. Wisely, she didn't introduce herself to me or shake my hand. That might not have been appropriate since Cohn and Engels hadn't introduced me. However, Sandra's smile and slight appropriate acknowledgment made me feel real good. Which, of course, made me feel real good about her. She got my vote.

She also got the job.

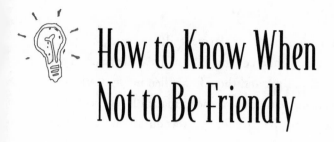

How to Know When Not to Be Friendly

Right after school, I worked at a small firm as the assistant to Darla, the public relations person. We became office friends, and, on her birthday, I took her to her favorite restaurant.

A few tables away, we spotted our company consultant, who came down to our department several times a week to chat with Darla. Tony was having lunch with a woman who was blonde, built for wow, and unmistakably not his wife. When Tony tenderly touched the lady's hand, I turned my chair away. But not Darla.

"Oh, there's Tony," she squealed in delight. "Let's go say hello to him!" Before I could stick my leg out to trip her, she made a beeline for his table. Her EP meter was obviously out of whack. She had missed the look of terror on Tony's face. Not wanting to witness the agonizing scene, I scurried off to the ladies' room.

When I returned, a stunned Darla was slumped back at our table. "I just don't understand it," she said. "Tony wasn't very friendly. Oh, well," she rationalized, "maybe he's just having a bad day."

He is now!

Tony didn't visit our department during the following month, and Darla wondered why. I didn't have the heart to tell her. Then one day, Tony and the CEO called me up to the top floor. Management wanted someone to make PR reports to the board and, of course, be paid for it. I was dumbfounded when they offered me the job.

I was about to suggest that Darla was more qualified when I had a blinding flash of the obvious. Tony didn't want anyone who had seen his clandestine rendezvous circulating around the top floor. I was "safe" because he didn't think I'd seen his little tryst.

I didn't get the promotion for what I knew. I got it for what Tony thought I didn't!

You've heard people say, "I saw it with my own eyes?" Emotional Prediction says, "No. See it through *their* eyes first. If it looks OK to them, then see it with your own eyes."

Little Trick #63
Don't Know "Too Much" About People

Often, it's not whom you know or even what you know. It can be what you know about whom you know. And about how much they know about what you know—and wish you didn't. Unless it's a potentially dangerous or legal matter, take a tip from the wise monkeys. They see no hanky-panky, hear no hanky-panky, speak of no hanky-panky.

Don't Always Listen to Your Friends

What you know about who you know—and how you found out—doesn't just concern promotions and professional relationships. You can lose friends by knowing too much about them—even if they tell you!

Tiffany was a founding member of our monthly girls' night out group, which we called "The Talking Tarts." She was great fun and we appreciated that she coordinated many of our get-togethers.

One Friday evening at a restaurant, Tiffany drank two too many. She started giggling and slurred, "I really live up to the, hic, club's name!" She then went on to tell us about an affair she was having with a local celebrity. "A *married* celebrity," she whispered loud enough for us all to hear.

She started giving details about their clandestine little trips out of town. Just as she was about to reveal his identity to her small breathless audience, Gabriella, one of the newer "Talking Tarts," tried to change the subject. But to no avail. Tiffany was too tipsy to be stopped.

Gabriella stood up to go to the ladies' room. When she returned and heard Tiffany still babbling on about her affair, Gabriella apologized and told us she had to get home early. She gave each of us a hug, including Tiffany, and left.

An almost tangible wave of respect for Gabriella swept over the table. She hadn't wanted to hear Tiffany's scandalous confession.

Tiffany wasn't at our next gathering, or our next. Everyone missed her but sensed, sadly, we'd seen her for the last time. We knew the reason. She would find being with us too painful because it would remind Tiffany of her drunken confession, an experience she deeply regretted.

If we had all been as wise as Gabriella, our original group would still be together. It takes a ton of self-discipline to stick to Little Trick 64. However, it's well worth it if you want to keep your friends or the friendship of your business colleagues—or your job!

LITTLE Trick #64
Shut Them Up—for Their Sake

Contrary to what many people believe, complete candor of the confession type does not strengthen friendships. It can destroy them. Perhaps, after a couple of beers one evening, your buddy starts to tell you something his sober self wouldn't. Be warm. Be friendly. But *don't* be a listener. Change the subject before he tells you too much. If he is unstoppable, leave.

Will he still like you in the morning, even though you walked out on his confessional story? *Yes*—even more than before!

Using the previous two Little Tricks, or not, can mean professional life or death in business. The next one can preserve your credibility.

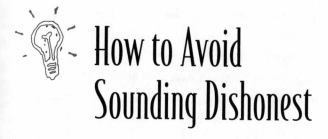

How to Avoid Sounding Dishonest

Whatever field you are in, your industry probably has conventions. And, of course, the participants go to learn something. For example, when doctors, dentists, and chiropractors go to their conferences, they want to gain knowledge from other docs. The crucial part of their presentations is the content.

Not so for my own arena, motivational speakers (who smugly prefer the designation "professional speaker"). In addition to the big voices, big mouths, and big egos that circulate at the industry convention, speakers make big judgments about each other. Not so much for content, but for style, stories, and originality. Everyone who speaks in the main auditorium at the National Speakers Association suffers merciless scrutiny from an acre of other loquacious types.

Several years ago, the association invited a celebrity speaker and well-known author of a series of bestselling books to give the keynote address. As soon as the doors opened, hundreds of speakers charged into the crowded ballroom, anxious get a sample of this gentleman's celebrated oratory.

True to expectation, the speaker kept the crowd spellbound. His energy and enthusiasm were unmatched. His gestures were exciting. He was a top professional in every sense. About fifteen minutes into his speech, he announced, "Here's a true story." We couldn't wait to hear it.

Big-Time Speaker made a grandiose gesture and began:

A powerful battleship is plowing through rough seas on a murky dark night. The captain peers out through the thick fog and perceives another light in the distance.

Some of the speakers looked bewildered because it had the ring of a story we had all heard before.

The captain blinks out an emergency message to warn the other ship. "Emergency! Collision inevitable! Change your course ten degrees to the north!"

By now, audience members were questioning each other in muted whispers. "Isn't this the old chestnut we've all heard?" We assumed it was a joke and he would soon give the punch line.

Our hopes faded further when he continued:

The light in the distance blinks back an answer. "Emergency! Collision inevitable! You change your course."

Now the captain of the big battleship gets angry and sends a Morse code message back. "No, you change YOUR course ten degrees to the north!" He frantically notifies the other captain about the size of his vessel, his guns, and the importance of his mission. He tells the other captain he has one option: "YOU MOVE OR GET BLOWN OUT OF THE WATER!"

At this point, disappointed audience members started to dribble out of the ballroom. Mr. Celebrity was telling an old standard speaker's story—and trying to convince them it was true.

In spite of the diaspora, Big-Time Speaker continued, as animated as ever:

The infuriated captain of the battleship repeats his message and adds, "I am captain of the biggest battleship in the fleet."

A reply signal came through the fog, "I am a lighthouse."

This powerful parable usually brings applause from even the toughest audiences when presented as a fable. This time, there was only a gratuitous smattering of clapping.

Had the big-time celebrity speaker prefaced it as a fictional story that made a powerful point, we would have enjoyed hearing it again—especially with his passion, gusto, and electric gestures. We left saddened, however, because we were no longer able to respect this icon. All because of the one sentence he uttered, "Here's a true story."

The Two Words That Destroyed Him

At dinner that night, a group of us was discussing the impact of saying something is a true story. One of our respected colleagues said, "I never use those words—even if it is a true story."

"Why?" we asked, almost in unison.

"Because it makes everybody think, 'He's telling us this story is true. Does that mean the rest of them aren't?'"

We discussed similar expressions like, "I'll be honest with you . . ." What does that subconsciously imply to your listeners? It tells them you haven't been truthful all along. Instead, you have decided, just for this one time, you are going to be honest.

Such phrases as "to tell you the truth" or "frankly speaking" insinuate the same thing. I call them "fibber phrases."

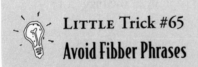

LITTLE Trick #65
Avoid Fibber Phrases

Sadly, even when the most truthful, trustworthy, decent, and law-abiding citizen uses phrases like "I'll be honest with you," and "frankly," people subconsciously suspect she is lying at other times. After all, why would she tout something as being the truth if everything she said really was? Don't run the risk of sounding fake. Eliminate fibber phrases.

Younger friends, this next one is for you!

How to Avoid Sounding Immature

I beg your indulgence while I get a personal gripe off my chest. Once done, I won't, *like*, mention it again in, *like*, this whole book. Can you, *like*, guess what I'm talking about?

Yes—the ubiquitous, overused, distressing, hackneyed, clichéd "like." To me, the word sounds like fingernails on a blackboard or a cat in a blender.

Just a few days ago, I was in the mall waiting in line to buy a DVD. Two girls behind me were gabbing away like squirrels on speed. Practically every other word they said was *like*. Sadistically, I decided to count them. I looked at my watch. It was 5:25 on the nose. I heard one girl say, "I was, like, bummed out. I, like, actually saw him with Cierra."

"How? Where were you?"

"Right here, I was, like, having my nails done at that salon over there."

"Oh no, Tina, I would have been, like, totally destroyed."

"I know, it was soooo weird. She's, like, the last girl I'd expect to see him with."

The *likes* were flying at me so fast and furiously I couldn't continue to count. My watch said 5:25:20.

I did the math: in one minute, I would hear their favorite word twenty-five times. I calculated if I were sentenced to listening to them for one hour, I would hear "like" fifteen hundred times!

What Were They Really Saying?

Everyone knows several synonyms for "like," such as "similar," "resembling," and "comparable." As I drove home, I sarcastically asked myself:

Was Tina bummed out or just something *similar* to being bummed out? Did she actually see her boyfriend with Cierra or something *akin to* seeing him with Cierra? Was she really having her nails done at the salon or just doing something *comparable to* having her nails done? Was Cierra really the last girl she expected to see him with or just someone *resembling* the last girl she would expect to see him with? In other words, she really wasn't saying anything real.

Reflect for a moment upon our valiant leaders in the twentieth century who have stirred hearts and upheld great ideals in the face of grave challenges—the figureheads who have led nations to new frontiers. What if they had spoken like Tina?

Imagine John Fitzgerald Kennedy's inaugural speech, January 20, 1961:

And so, my fellow Americans: ask not what your country can, *like*, do for you. Ask what you can, *like*, do for your country. . . . With, *like*, a good conscience our only sure reward, with history, *like*, the final judge of our deeds, let us go forth to, *like*, lead the land we love.

Enough said?

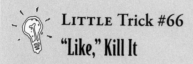

LITTLE Trick #66
"Like," Kill It

Don't sound as though you are saying something similar to, equal to, or resembling the truth. Communicate that you are speaking facts, not, "like," you are speaking facts.

Incidentally, Tina might not feel so cool and au courant when she learns the slang use of *like* originated in the 1930s—along with "hepcat" and "twenty-three skidoo." Don't let your vocabulary be, like, whoa . . . whatever.

How to Avoid Big Cats Considering You Commonplace

You have every right to disagree with the following. Many very nice people do. In fact, I haven't yet decided whether I agree with it. But I would be remiss in not reporting on a particular prejudice that flows in the veins of the more evolved of our species. They cringe when they hear—are you ready? *Have a nice day.* One of them told me, "To me, it sounds like a little cat vomiting."

When an innocent bystander to intelligent life bestows this sentiment, kinder big cats merely mutter the obligatory "You, too" and promptly forget the words that offended their selective ears—and the person who uttered them.

Understandably, many smaller cats who have crinkled their whiskers trying to crack the glass ceiling feel this attitude is elitist. "How superficial and snooty," they meow.

They are right. Many good-hearted people genuinely want you to have a nice day. They express this sincere sentiment to their friends, family members, acquaintances, customers, vendors, and sometimes even to passersby.

So why do the big winners react so negatively to "Have a nice day?" I pondered this deep sociological question. After much reflection, I surmised that the first few thousand times they heard it, it warmed their hearts.

Now they recoil because they hear a constant cacophony of "have-a-nice-day, you-too" lethargically chanted by customers, cashiers, taxi drivers, grocery clerks, ad infinitum. They usually accompany it with no smile, no eye contact, no articulation, and no emotion. In fact, sometimes it's so gruff that it sounds like a mutual death threat.

At five one morning, while writing this book, I succumbed to my common craving for a Diet Coke. Because I was trying to go cold turkey on the noxious carbonated fluid, there was none in the fridge. In a fit of self-hatred and ruminating on how Coke can rust a penny, I jumped into my jeans and raced down to the twenty-four-hour deli.

I paid the guy behind the cash register and, unscrewing my king-size Diet Coke as I left, I heard . . . nothing. Silence. I had come to expect the trite valediction at the conclusion of every business transaction. As a lighthearted joke, I turned around and said to him, "Hey, aren't you going to tell me to have a nice day?"

Without lifting his eyes off the cash register, he grumbled, "It's on the 'effen' receipt."

I clasped my Coke and increased my pace.

Old Habits Are Hard to Quit!

Every time we say the same thing, it chisels the groove deeper in our grey matter. I once met the receptionist of the Los Angeles

entertainment law firm that represented, among other lumi-
naries, Tom Hanks, Harrison Ford, and Eddie Murphy. She
told me if her home phone rang at 3:00 A.M., instead of saying
"hello," she would answer, "Ziffren, Brittenham, Branca, Fischer, Gilbert-Lurie, Stiffelman, Cook, Johnson, Lande & Wolf.
How may I direct your call?" If the sleepy girl cannot prevent
mechanically muttering twenty-one syllables, it's certainly not
easy to evade the hackneyed four, "Have a nice day."

So What's the Solution?

Rehearse! Rehearse! Rehearse! Replace the "Have a nice day"
groove in your brain with a variety of others such as:

> "Enjoy your day."
> "Have a pleasant day."
> "I hope you have a good day."
> "Enjoy the rest of your day."

Hearing anything other than that routine four-syllable
cliché makes someone feel special, as though—surprise,
surprise!—you actually notice that he is a human being! Your
reward will be his smile.

Little Trick #67
Decimate "Have a Nice Day."

I sincerely hope that, by the time you are reading this, "Have a nice day" will have gone wherever old overused phrases, like "See you later, alligator / In a while, crocodile," go rest in peace, never to be invoked again except by historians. If not, force yourself to resist saying the four syllables that brand you as banal. Replace them with one of the more original (by comparison) phrases above.

How Should I Respond When Someone Says, "Have a Nice Day?"

If they hurl the hackneyed "Have a nice day" at you, bite your tongue and resist the sardonic urge to say:

"Thanks, but I have other plans."
"Don't tell me how to live my life."
"Gee, I was planning on having a miserable one, but now that you mention it, I think I'll have a nice one."

Simply smile at them and respond, "You, too." Then revel in the knowledge that you are a more evolved Homo sapien and wouldn't have spit out the stock four-word greeting that makes you sound unoriginal.

Here are a few more common quickies that you should edit out of your big cat vocabulary.

How to Avoid Common Dumb Phrases People Say All the Time

I don't remember ever leaving a seminar feeling more dejected. It was more painful than the time I mooned the audience of attorneys.

I was giving one of several concurrent sessions at a convention. As is often customary, the convention organizers placed an easel just outside each seminar room door with the name of the program and a picture of the presenter on it.

An effervescent young woman arrived early. As she sat down, she said, "Oh, Ms. Lowndes, that is a wonderful photograph of you on the easel!" I gave her the obligatory thank-you, but it felt like a jab below the belt. I am sure she meant it as a compliment, but it implied, "The photo looks better than you do."

Well, OK, maybe I'm being paranoid. That's probably just her opinion.

Then another participant who came in right after her said, "It really is a great shot. When was it taken?" OUCH! That was an excruciating uppercut. I managed to get through the seminar, but I emerged from it punch drunk. I threw in the towel on that photo and got a new one.

If you open your mouth and find those cruel words "That's a great photo of you" slipping out, rapidly rescue your listener's ego by saying something like, "but it doesn't do you justice." Or maybe, "It really captures your essence."

Whenever complimenting anyone on appearances, first run it through your EP meter. Some people feel too old, too young, too fat, too thin, too short, too tall . . . the list goes on. Compliments like, "That makes you look younger/taller/slender" could be a hit below the belt.

Just the other day, I heard a knock on my door.

"Who is it?" I asked.

"Fed-Ex" a loud voice shouted back.

Being hesitant to let him in, I checked him out through my door peephole. A young man with a lovely face was holding a package. Opening the door, I "complimented" him—or so I thought—by saying, "You don't look so scary."

His sweet, innocent face fell and he said sadly, "Yeah, I'm just a little guy." I felt terrible. Never forget the "Paranoia Principle." Keep adjusting your EP antenna so it picks up any possibility that that your comments could cut into someone's ego. Practically everybody takes everything personally.

By the way, never preface any sentence with "Don't take this personally." You know they will.

Here are a few more "Don't Says":

- **"I'm sorry, I just didn't have time . . . (fill in: to call, to write, and so on)."** Upon hearing this, the listener's hypothalamus tells her cerebellum, *"Who does he think he's kidding? He had time to eat, sleep, go to the bathroom, socialize, and make a dozen phone calls this week. That puts me at the very bottom of his list."*

- **"Have a safe flight!"** Sometimes even this most innocent phrase can freak people out. People sincerely believe they are being thoughtful when they tell someone just before he boards the plane, "Have a safe flight." However, some people have told me that this stirs a subconscious fear: *"Hmm. Maybe the flight won't be safe. I could get killed in a plane crash! Besides, what the heck can I do? Go tell the pilot!"*
- **"Drive safely!"** She thinks: *"Oh, gee, thanks for telling me. I was planning to drive dangerously."*
- **"Have a safe trip home."** When you extend these good wishes, New Yorkers have fantasies of subway stabbings, park rapes, and purse robbers.
- **"No problem!"** He wonders: *"You mean you usually do have a problem with people? And it's so rare that you don't that you need to announce it?"*
- **"Don't trip."** He speculates: *"Does she think I'm that clumsy?"*
- **"You look great!"** She frets: *"You mean I didn't yesterday?"*

 Little Trick #68
Avoid Thoughtless Common Comments

Before giving someone a good wish, ponder how his paranoid mind (and who doesn't have one?) might translate it. Whenever you give someone a compliment, think it through first. Be sensitive to the fact that it can invoke bad fantasies or a negative self-image.

People get a negative gut reaction that bypasses their consciousness. Why kick them in the gut?

How to Avoid Alienating Friends When Traveling

I find the following Little Trick a bit jaded, but a big cat whom I respect asked me to include it. I ignored her suggestion . . . until a few days later. Something happened that, temporarily at least, blew away my hesitancy. So here it is.

I had been writing around the clock, getting dangerously close to the deadline on this book. It was winter, and the heat in my loft wasn't sufficient. Lest carpal tunnel syndrome set in my shivering wrists, I took a quick break to go to the mailbox.

Inside, I found two postcards from friends I hadn't heard from in months. One was from "Heavenly Hawaii" and the other from the French Rivera. Great, just what I needed when it was nineteen degrees outside.

One card said, "Thinking of you" (when I know the sender wasn't). The other friend had written, "Wish you were here," which she *definitely* didn't. No matter what the postcards said, they seemed to tauntingly shout, "See how much fun I'm having in this glorious paradise? You're stuck in the snow at home. Don't you envy me?"

As I clutched their malevolent cards in my Gore-Tex gloves, I cynically thought, *Sure, if you're really thinking of me, spring for*

223

a phone call to say "hi." At the very least, send me an e-mail with a longer personalized message. Don't mail me a ten-cent picture of a destination you want me to envy. In seven-tenths of a second, I could find four hundred thousand prettier ones on the Web. Besides, you haven't been in touch with me in months. Why show off now?

I know it sounds cruel and unfair. But when I pressured a few refined individuals for their opinions on sending postcards, they agreed. Sending a postcard to someone you talk to every week is understandable. If you haven't communicated with someone in over a month, though, why take a chance that your friends might think you're showing off? Or worse, they could interpret it as saying, "Look where I am. Eat your heart out."

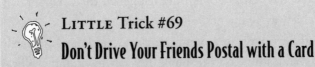

LITTLE Trick #69
Don't Drive Your Friends Postal with a Card

If you send postcards to seldom-seen friends when you're on vacation, you do so at your own risk. If you're really thinking of them and not just showing off, be sure to e-mail them a personal message as well. If it's really a good friend, call from Enviable Location and say, "I was thinking of you this morning. How great if you could be here with me." It's a lot more convincing by e-mail or phone.

Here is something else a big cat might find in his or her mailbox that wouldn't have a return address from somewhere above the glass ceiling.

How to Avoid a Common Holiday Custom That Makes You Look like a Little Puss to Big Cats

You might be tempted to file this Little Trick in the "Snooty" drawer. I was stunned to discover, however, the sentiment is surprisingly common. All I ask is that you hear me out and then make your own decision.

Reality check: Most big cats hiss at an annual photocopied holiday letter. As they read it, they are disdainfully thinking, *This sender assumes everyone is salivating to hear all about their family's magnificent accomplishments in the past 365 days.*

Some happy holiday writers even apologize that their letter is late—signifying their certitude that the recipient is concerned that they have not received it yet and checks the mailbox for it daily.

The Annual "From Our Family to Yours" Letter

Here is a typical family Christmas or holiday letter. The parts in parentheses indicate how a big cat recipient might react.

Dear friends, this has been a very special year for us. Dad, because of his great knowledge of his field, has decided to become a consultant.

He lost his job and no one else would hire him.

So that our son can be closer to us, Johnny has chosen to go to the community college nearby.

Every university he applied to turned him down.

And, the biggest news of all, we have a grandchild on the way. Our oldest daughter is expecting a bundle of joy in March.

They don't mention that her husband walked out on her six months ago, and she has now filed a paternity suit against the postman.

We pray that you and yours have had a wonderful year, too.

 LITTLE Trick #70
Think Before Sending an Annual Holiday Letter

I don't mean to sound like Scrooge. However, as your humble journalist, I feel obligated to report the facts: Many big cats chuck photocopied Christmas letters in the wastebasket, unread. Before they do that, however, they note the sender's name so they can add it to their little puss list.

PART EIGHT

ELEVEN LITTLE TRICKS

to Give Your E-Mail Today's Personality and Tomorrow's Professionalism

How to Prove You Are Special When You Are Out of the Office

I have often wondered why human beings transform themselves into androids in their automated out-of-the-office messages. Except for changing the names, here is one I recently received.

> This is an automatically generated acknowledgment of your e-mail. I am currently out of the office until April 1 and cannot be reached. However, this is to inform you that your message has been received and, upon my return, I will respond in due course.
>
> If you should require immediate assistance in my absence, contact my assistant, Gina Gynoid, at extension 702, who may be able to assist you.
>
> If you are a spammer, take me off your list.
>
> Roberta Robot

Come on Roberta, flesh-and-blood people don't talk like that! Scrap the banana republic formality and get real.

Let's Dissect Her Message

"This is an automatically generated acknowledgment of your e-mail."

Oh, that's a great start. Nobody wants to feel they are reading a lifeless computer's cold reply. Why rub it in that it is "automatically generated"?

"I am currently out of the office . . ."

D'uh, it's obviously "current."

" . . . and cannot be reached."

Are you a prisoner of war in solitary confinement in a remote country that has no communication with the outside world? What if there is an emergency? "Cannot be reached" sounds ominous.

"This is to inform you . . ."

That sounds like the opening of a subpoena.

"Upon my return . . ."

Is that English? I have never heard anyone put it that way verbally. What about "When I return"? Or even, "When I get back"?

"I will respond in due course."

When is "due course"? Next week? Next fiscal year? Next decade? Are you telling me that you must first respond to a long line of more important messages before mine comes up "in due course"?

"If you should require immediate assistance in my absence . . ."

First of all, Roberta, "assistance" is too formal. Most people just say "help." But that's not ideal either, because most of us don't need help. We are healthy human beings who are merely contacting you for a reason. Just say, "If you need something while I'm away . . ."

"Contact my assistant, Gina Gynoid, at extension 702, who may be able to assist you."

"May" be able to assist me? That's encouraging. Replace it with, "She will assist you . . ." Gina will tell me if she can't.

"If you are a spammer, take me off your list."

Now how dumb is that? You think spammers will assiduously read the details of your out-of-the-office message and say, "Oh darn, Roberta, you don't want us to contact you anymore? OK, we'll take you off our list."

Have Real Intelligence, Not Artificial Intelligence

To make yourself sound like the living, eating, breathing Homo sapien that you are, try something like this the next time you are away.

> Thank you for your message. I am away until April 1 and will answer you when I get back. Contact Gina Gynoid, my assistant, at extension 702 if you need anything before then. Looking forward to being in touch when I return.

And, if you want to sound really professional, yet warm, change the subject line from "Out of the office" to "I am away until April 1."

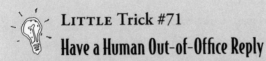

Little Trick #71
Have a Human Out-of-Office Reply

Why mimic a machine when you can sound like
a mortal? You wouldn't write "All articles that
coruscate with resplendence are not truly auriferous,"
when you mean "all that glitters is not gold."

Don't be stiff in your out-of-the-office reply when
it's even easier to be friendly. It's no less professional
to write your out-of-the-office message the way you'd
say it.

How to Make People Smile When They See Your Message

You have probably heard the story of Ivan Petrovich Pavlov's pooches salivating at the sound of a bell. You may not, however, have heard of his other slobbering dogs. I find that experiment more memorable, and you might, too, so let us go with the other canine study.

Pavlov originally served his canine subjects gourmet meals coated with chili powder. After a while, he denied them their epicurean delights and just sprinkled some chili powder around. Yet, for a long time, his dogs continued to drool at the smell of chili powder. It's called "being conditioned."

You needn't condition your e-mail recipients to drool when they see the message is from you, but nor do you want them to shudder.

A few years ago, I took care of my two young nieces for a week while their parents took a long-awaited and much deserved vacation. I had to leave for an overnight trip, but a reliable friend, Fiona, offered to stay with them at my place.

The next morning, at the hotel, just before my speech, I received an e-mail from her. The subject line was "Accident." *!!!!!!!*

My fingers shook so violently, I had trouble opening the message. It read, "Oh, Leil, I feel so awful. I knocked over that beautiful green vase you have in the living room and it shattered. I tried to glue it, but it will never be the same again. . . ."

Nor would my feelings for Fiona. Not consciously, that is. And not because of the vase, but because of the jolt she'd given me. She obviously didn't predict my emotion—the terror I would feel after reading her subject line.

Now, every time I see Fiona's name in the "From" field, I involuntarily shudder. She inadvertently conditioned me to feel fear just seeing that the message is from her. Didn't she realize that I'd freak out just reading the word *accident* when my precious little nieces, Allison and Julia, were in her care?

Think about it. How would you feel getting an e-mail from your boss with the following subject line? "Meet me in my office at nine tomorrow morning." Even if Boss's message said he wanted to give you a raise, the momentary jolt would have already done its damage.

No matter what good tidings your messages bear, predict the emotions of recipients reading the subject line. The fleeting pain pricks you gave them are hard to erase.

LITTLE Trick #72
Avoid Scary Subject Lines

Be careful that your subject line couldn't be misunderstood and inadvertently foreshadow something negative. No matter what pleasantries follow in your message, it's too late. Your recipient has *subconsciously* anchored you to unpleasantness. Forever after, just seeing your name in the "From" field reinvokes that painful jolt.

The Opposite Is True, Too

Conversely, the subject line "You got a raise!" translates into warm feelings for Boss.

Always anchor yourself to pleasure by writing upbeat subject lines. For example, if someone has given you a gift, write "Fabulous gift!" as the subject. If you are writing someone to say how much you enjoyed her party, write "Great Party!" Why make your recipients wait until they get into the message to get a smile?

When I sent the manuscript of this book to my editor, her first message back was "Love it!" Unfortunately, it turns out she had only read the table of contents. But Judith's subject line thrilled me so much that I kept it going on our messages for months—even when she was scolding me about a part she didn't like!

What if the Subject Thread Is Already Established?

If the same ol' subject line has been going back and forth, leave it as is. When appropriate though, add an upbeat comment after it in parentheses. Let's say your team at the office has been working on a project for the Patton company and the e-mail thread has been "The Patton Project." Now it is successfully over. Keep the original subject, and add the make 'em smile part: "RE: The Patton Project (Great job everybody!)"

Do you ever watch reruns of the classic sitcom "Seinfeld"? Kramer's scenes are so funny that audiences laugh the second he skids in the door—before he even says a word. Do the same thing with your subject lines. Check your "Sent" mailbox now, and scan your old subject lines. How many of them would make your recipient smile before opening the message?

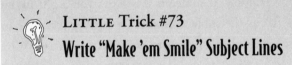

LITTLE Trick #73

Write "Make 'em Smile" Subject Lines

Starting today, write only upbeat subject lines. If the subject is already established, season it occasionally with something pleasant in parentheses. After you send a few of these make 'em smile subject lines, you have conditioned people to have a warm response to just seeing that a message is from you.

I've often heard people say that e-mail is impersonal and that you can't tell much about someone just from their written words. I beg to differ. Naturally, your messages don't reveal as much as your voice or your body language. But your words are like a lighthouse signaling everyone about your self-image.

How to Make Your E-Mail Sound Confident

Here are three common e-mail messages:

> Hi Jenna, I was hoping that you'd be free for dinner Friday night.—Geoffrey
> Hi Kelly, I thought it would be a good idea to call the client this afternoon.—Asuka
> LaTonya, I wanted to know when you'd like the proposal finished.—Connor

Question: How can you tell that each of these writers feels lower on the totem pole than the person he's writing to?

Answer: Geoffrey, Asuka, and Connor put their desires in the *past tense*, which makes them sound timid making their requests. Besides, it doesn't make sense. Is Geoffrey so timid about asking Jenna to dinner that he has to sound like he *no longer cares*?

Does it mean that Asuka *thought* it would be a good idea to call the client but no longer does? Does Connor *no longer* want to know about his boss's wishes? When you speak or write in the past tense, you weaken your point or question. It reeks of insecurity.

You "were hoping"? No! Say, "I *hope* you will be . . ."

You "thought it was a good idea"? No! Say, "I *think* it's a good idea . . ."

You "wanted to know"? No! Say, "I *want* to know . . ."

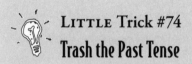

LITTLE Trick #74
Trash the Past Tense

Don't talk in the insecure past tense. Speak in the confident present. Would Mom say to her messy kid, "I wanted you to clean up your room"? Would a hopeful husband-to-be get down on one knee and say to his ladylove, "I wanted you to marry me"? What is this lame past-tense stuff? Trash it now and forever.

A quick note for my sisters: When writing to men, drop words that express how you feel, like:

"I am thrilled that . . ."

"I am so happy that . . ."

"That made me feel so (whatever)."

Remember, men don't have feelings. At least, most of them don't admit it!

Then there's the flip side, those who sound *too* confident, i.e., smug and self-centered.

How to Avoid Sounding Egotistical in Your E-Mail

People who reside in mental institutions use the word *I* twelve times more than "nonresidents." Ergo, it figures that the fewer times you use the word *I*, the saner you sound.

In conversation, it's certainly a good idea to avoid saying *I* too many times. Once uttered, though, it becomes just another sound wave blown away by the breezes. In e-mail, however, that big black *I* stays plastered on your recipient's screen. Some people start so many sentences with *I* that their message looks like it has a left-hand border.

Wait a minute, Leil. Everybody talks about themselves—their actions, thoughts, feelings, suggestions. That's what messages are all about.

You are right. In fact, here is a typical casual message to a friend:

Hi Ric, I really had a good time at your party last night at the club and met many interesting people. I hope you and your wife can join us next week for dinner. I think you will enjoy Sasha's cooking.

Notice how an *I* starts each sentence? They're repetitive, not to mention self-focused, even though the writer is supposedly reaching out to his friend.

So what is an e-mailer to do? If dearly deceased Miss Peasgood heard the following advice, she would turn over in her grave. If she were alive, it would drive her to it. But it's simple to do. Just delete the word *I* as much as possible. Let's try it and see how it sounds.

> Hi Ric, really had a good time at your party last night at the club and met many interesting people. Hope you and your wife can join us next week for dinner. Think you will enjoy Sasha's cooking.

This one used precisely the same words as the first, just deleting the word *I*. There isn't one of them in the entire message.

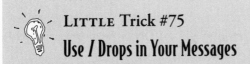

LITTLE Trick #75
Use *I* Drops in Your Messages

Tweak your informal e-mails and wipe out the word *I* as many times as you can. You will sound less self-centered—and therefore more likable. To prove it, open any e-mail message you have recently written. Delete practically every *I*, and the message will probably stand on its own. Everybody will like it better, except grammarians.

In spots where it sounds strange to drop the *I*, simply put *your recipient's* name before it: "Ric, I hope you and your wife can join us . . ."

If you'd like to take it a step further, switch the words around to start as many sentences as you can with *you*.

> Hi Ric, *you* really gave a great party last night at the club, and everyone enjoyed it. *You* invited a lot of interesting people. *You* and *your* wife can join us for dinner next week, right? *You'll* enjoy Sasha's cooking.

Business E-Mail

Substituting *you* for *I* makes business communications friendlier, too. See which you like better:

> Dear Mr. Jones: We received your order for two gizmos yesterday. I will e-mail you as soon as they come, and we will send them out the day after.

That's average, the way people usually write messages. Here's the "Little Trick #75" way to write it:

> Dear Mr. Jones: *Your* order for two gizmos arrived yesterday. *You* will be notified by e-mail as soon as they come in, and *you* will receive them the day after.

Reread some of your old e-mail messages to see how many sentences you could have turned around to start with the word *you*. Then pretend you are the recipient of that message, not the sender. Do you see the difference?

If your messages that make them feel important pile up, you've got yourself a loyal customer.

From the time the doctor holds newborns upside down by their tiny feet and spanks them, all of them feel the world revolves around them. For their entire lives, hearing you say their name or the word *you* gives them a pleasure-pat. Here's how to give them an even bigger stroke.

How to Sound like You Have a Crystal Ball

Before every flight, airline pilots do a pretakeoff check of how much fuel is in the tank and whether the wing flaps move freely. Likewise, before your e-mail messages take off into cyberspace, perform a relationship check.

Practically all civilized folk make a gratuitous, almost obligatory reference to the recipient in their opening sentence, such as "Hope you had a good weekend." Or they extend their good wishes for holidays past, present, or future. That's as original as a white wall.

Thanks to the wonders of the World Wide Web, you can now make your messages more relevant. Let's say you are writing to someone in a different state. Check the local weather report. Did she just have:

A big snowstorm? "Hi Brenda, How are you surviving the blizzard?"
A wildfire? "Natalie, I do hope that horrible blaze didn't get anywhere near your neighborhood."
A heat wave? "Hey, girl, did you melt yet?"

The recipients will never guess that weather.com did the work for you. Keep it on your favorites list.

What's the Big News from Their Berg?

Tack a world map on your wall. Now, throw a dart at it. Wherever it lands, no matter how tiny the town, something has happened there. You've never seen a banner headline, even in the *One Horse Herald*, saying "Nothing Happened Here Today."

Is a celebrity visiting their boonies? Did the hometown boy genius win third place in the state spelling bee? What about the grand opening of the new museum of twentieth-century beer bottle caps?

Your reader will never suspect the obvious, that your Web search gave you the skinny. You only spent a few seconds to score big with them.

Narrow It Down Even Further

The recipient doesn't have to be from out of town to use this Little Trick. Your search engine can surreptitiously swoop down on every neighborhood and dig up any dirt that a freaked-out blogger has written about their 'hood.

I once received an e-mail from an uptown colleague who wrote, "Hope no falling bricks hit you." He was referring to a freshly fallen building in my lower Manhattan neighborhood. This is a common and unnoteworthy event in the Big Bagel. Unless it's yours or a neighbor's building.

His knowledge and concern impressed me.

> ## Little Trick #76
> ### Do a News and Weather Check Before Sending
>
> Take just a few seconds to enhance or create a relationship with your recipient. Send your search engine into cyberspace like a St. Bernard and, before you blink, it will be back with something better than a barrel of brandy to boost your connection. It's a small investment for a big reward.

What if There Is No News "Fit to Print"?

All is not lost. Run a search for their many-months-ago e-mails to find something to refer to.

> "Zach, you never told me about your drive to Disneyland last year. Did the kids enjoy it?"
>
> "Nora, how's that new little niece of yours doing? Get to spend much time with her?"
>
> "Kaylie—did you ever discover the identity of your mystery admirer who sent you the rock candy? What did the dentist say?"

> **LITTLE Trick #77**
> ## Put Memories in Your Messages
>
> Take a diving expedition into previous messages from
> your intended recipient. Surface with some forgettable
> (to everybody but them) fact about their life—and
> refer to it. They think, *"Wow, I must really be important
> to her. Look how she remembers the details of my life!"*

Be an Archaeologist

Still didn't find anything? Don't give up. Excavate any other
elements you can refer to. Check the time he sent the message
and, if it is atypical in any way, refer to it. Did he send you a
business communication at 7:00 A.M. or 7:00 P.M. from the
office? End your message with, "Go home, Christopher. You're
working too hard!"

She sent it at the wee hours? Jokingly chastise her, "You're
burning the midnight oil again, Madison. Go get some beauty
sleep." (Do not imply that she needs it, of course.)

Even their initials. My friend Eleanor signs her messages
with an adorable "x e," meaning "Kisses, Eleanor." Another
friend, Bob Summers, signs his e-mail with just his initials.
But I don't comment on that one.

A Digging Expedition for Diehards

What if there is no unusual weather, no news, no old messages, no weird sending time? If you don't want to give up on

personalizing their message, here's a last-ditch effort. (I know, I know, this is really stretching it, but . . .) Is there a colored background behind the message? Did they write it in an unusual font, say Batang Sans Serif or Mongolian Baiti Condensed? Compliment it, if you can decipher it.

How to Avoid Making People Think You're Goofing Off at Work

No doubt you have heard people pompously proclaim, "Me? Oh no. I *never* watch television." What do you want to bet that, when no one is looking, they lock the door, pull the blinds, and watch "The Young and the Restless" or "Bikini Babes."

It's the same at work. When someone receives an e-mail joke, who hasn't nervously glanced around to assure one is looking and then succumbed to temptation?

Sure, we all send jokes now and then, but senders beware. Many smart, serious folks glance at the *time* it arrived. If the funny makes touchdown on their screen between nine and five o'clock Monday through Friday, their esteem for the sender shrinks.

If you have something not related to business, hold it and don't click "send" before 6:00 P.M. It doesn't have to be a joke. It can be a sentimental story, a save the seals sermon, a warning about a nasal polyps plague, or photos of your baby from your wedding.

If your joke or even your personal message arrives during work hours, it is obvious to the recipient you are ripping off your boss. Anyone who screws around on company time—and then flaunts it—goes down a notch in practically everybody's estimation.

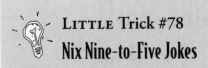

Little Trick #78
Nix Nine-to-Five Jokes

Why advertise you're goofing off at work? If you receive a gag during business hours, resist the temptation to forward it to your friends until after work. Envision yourself as their boss. Picture yourself above the glass ceiling looking down disdainfully at the sender. Now you are thinking like the big boys and girls.

Don't Step on People's Egos

Some years ago, when the send-a-joke epidemic was just starting to spread, I had a Saturday night date with great guy named Palmer. Imagine my thrill when I arrived at work on Monday morning and found a message from him. I anxiously opened it. Instead of a personal note telling me how much he enjoyed the date and how fabulous I was, it was a joke. My name was buried in a long list of other recipients. I was crushed. If only Palmer had personalized it with one sentence, "Leil, I thought you would enjoy seeing this," I might have had a second date with him.

Even better, he could have sent an accompanying personal message: "Leil, I occasionally send out things I find humorous. I hope you don't mind my adding your name to the list."

 LITTLE Trick #79
Ask Before Adding Their Name to Your Jokes Recipients List

If you occasionally do mass e-mailings—that means to any more than four friends—personalize it the first time you send one to a new person. Otherwise, you make him feel nameless, which means he might want to forget yours.

Even better, ask if he'd like to be a recipient. Whatever his answer, you will go up in his esteem, and he'll be waiting for your first communiqué.

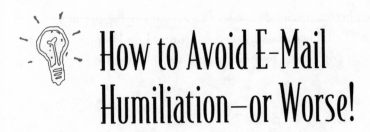

How to Avoid E-Mail Humiliation—or Worse!

When archaeologists open the time capsule from the 1950s, they will find tabletop jukeboxes, Clarabelle's seltzer bottle from the "Howdy Dowdy Show," a Brownie camera, a ten-inch black-and-white TV, a few 45 rpm records, and an embalmed Fuller Brush man. However, one item in the airtight capsule will totally confound them if they are under thirty.

What Is It?

Here is a clue: It is two pages of paper, eight and a half inches wide, eleven inches long, and glued together at the top. The top page is white and feels like tissue. The bottom is black. It is dull on one side, shiny on the other. If you touch it, you get black smudges on your fingers.

Generation Y readers, are you still stumped?

The Answer

Your elders called it "carbon paper." You put it into a type-writer with the dull black side facing you. (Millennials, you will find the definition of "typewriter" in your favorite online encyclopedia.)

You then rolled the paper in and typed on it. Voilà! You had a tissue copy of whatever you were writing. The last step was to go wash the carbon off your hands.

Carbon Copies, Twenty-First-Century Style

Although technology is moving faster than a speeding microprocessor, these days you still put a disclosed corecipient's name in a field called "CC" for "carbon copy" and the names of undisclosed recipients in a "BCC" field for "blind carbon copy."

Therein lies a problem. Message recipients seldom glance at who else has received a copy, and countless awkward situations can result. The most common is looking like a nitwit as you excitedly inform people of something they have already been CC'd on.

Whenever you are copying others on your message, type "CC" under your signature and list the names of others who are receiving it. It looks extra cool, like you're taking extra care that your recipient knows who else is reading your message.

How to Avoid Your Computer Getting You Fired

Here is a more important "CC." This one stands for "Check your Chain" (of messages) before copying someone else.

Now for a sad short story, with only the names changed. Carole was a colleague at a company I once worked for, and our supervisor (whom she detested) was Danielle.

One Monday, Carole e-mailed me a spoof on the beautiful poem Robert Browning sent to his beloved Elizabeth Barrett, "How do I love thee? Let me count the ways." Carole wrote, "How do I despise thee, Danielle? Let me count the ways." She followed it with an unexpurgated list of why she loathed our supervisor.

Carole and I continued e-mailing on work matters that week. And, of course, the poem went back and forth at the bottom of our thread of messages.

On Friday, Carole had to send Danielle a copy of the business project we had been working on. After reading her email (CC'd to Danielle), I glanced down our thread of messages and realized she had neglected to delete her "poem" frying Danielle—who was probably reading it at that moment.

Carole was conspicuously absent that following Monday—and every day after that.

If you listen carefully on a clear night in Silicon Valley, you will hear the chuckles of programmers blowing across the sand dunes. They have heard thousands of stories of love lost and jobs vanishing because of what users call "computer errors."

LITTLE Trick #80
Check CCs and Your "Chain" Before Sending

Whenever you are sending a message, scan the previous messages glued to it underneath. Take out anything you wouldn't post on the company or community bulletin board. If the wrong person reads your old message, she may decide you're in the wrong job.

Also, whenever you are copying others on your message, type "CC" under your signature and list the names of others who are receiving it. It is more professional and forthright, and it could save the recipient from looking like a nitwit. Not to mention that it looks very impressive.

To BCC or Not to BCC

Pompous professionals scorn the use of blind copies (BCC). They deem it "sneaky" if the recipient doesn't know who else received the message. Ergo, no serious book on communication skills should encourage the use of the BCC field. So let's pretend I'm not.

But, hey, sometimes you just gotta let someone know something that the someone being written to shouldn't know the other someone knows.

Any questions?

Disclaimer

If you send someone a blind carbon copy and suffer any loss, damage, or expense arising therefrom, in any form or in any written media, thereof, now known or hereafter developed, you indemnify Leil Lowndes, her heirs, executors, administrators, successors, and assigns from any responsibility from giving the BCC her blessing.

Now we come to one of the major challenges of savvy twenty-first-century e-mailers.

How to Sign Your Messages in the New Millennium

E-mail's official birthday is October 1971. Can you believe, these many years after the dawning of this universal technology, that we are still struggling with how to sign our messages? Should we write, "Regards"? "Sincerely"? "Best"? "Thanks"? Our name? Initials? Nothing? Babies born pre-Windows are totally bewildered. Those weaned on floppy disks are just as baffled.

When Generation Nexters ask their grandmother, "Granny, what are letters?" she will explain they were e-mail messages that were handwritten or keyboarded on paper. When she tells her grandchildren that every one of them had to be signed with "Sincerely yours," "Cordially yours," "Respectfully yours," and the like, they will stare at her in disbelief.

It finally dawned upon e-mail writers that using those valedictions mimicked archaic typewritten letters too much. Many shortened it to just one word, "Sincerely." Now we're even struggling to do away with that in more casual communicating.

Some people ask, "What about just signing your name? The majority answers, "That sounds callous."

Consulting the Shrink from Cyberspace

For the answer to the burning question, "How shall we sign our e-mails?" earthlings must summon the Great IT Man in the Sky to our planet. He is the cyberpsychiatrist who can answer perplexing psychological and ethical questions that come with the new technology.

The crowd stands, straining their necks to see Cyber Shrink's spaceship arrive. The moment he disembarks, there is a great crescendo of, "How should we sign our messages?"

Like all psychiatrists, he answers their question with a question: "Why must you have a closing to your message?"

"To pay deference to the receiver," someone shouts out. "It's so our messages have a friendlier ending."

"Yes," Cyber Shrink nods. He then points his finger in the air. "What is the sweetest sound in the English language to someone?"

"Their name?" the group asks.

He strokes his goatee and nods. "Yes, and that, my dear earthlings, is how you should sign your e-mail."

A few of the more confident in the crowd cry out, "What do *their* names have to do with *my* signature?"

Cyber Shrink again responds with a question. "The whole point of your signature phrase is to show respect and close your message in a friendly way, right?"

The throng nods in unison.

"So simply end your message with a warm sentence that includes their name. It is even better if you can make their name the very last word in the body of the message. That gives them what I believe you humans call 'the fuzzies and warms.' Then *your* name isn't necessary.

"In all but the most formal messages," he adds, "you can put your initials to signal that is the end. Alternatively, if you are especially attached to your first name, I condone that as well."

The grateful assembly gasps, "Yes, yes! Thank you!"

The wise guru then climbs back aboard his spaceship. The crowd looks up to the sky and waves as Cyber Shrink vanishes back into the universe where our e-mail gets lost.

Your Signature Is *Their* Name

Most people start an e-mail with the recipient's name: "Hi Heather," "Hey, Javier," "Aidan," and the like.) It's still appropriate to do that, but also end the message with that special word they love to hear. Here are some examples of how to sign your e-mail by working with their name:

"Thanks so much for your help, Samantha."
"I'm looking forward to talking with you, Nicholas."
"Lauren, it was lovely having dinner with you."
"Good going, Emma, you really impressed the client."
"It was a great meeting you, Maia."

Your initials, first name, or even nothing after such sentences suffice. Hearing their own name unexpectedly as the last word of your message makes them feel an instant connection with you.

By the time you read this book, mental telepathy may have replaced e-mail. However, that presents another problem. If we could read each other's minds, men and women would never get together to copulate. Our species would die out, and there would be no more need for e-mail.

Little Trick #81
Sign Your Messages with *Their* Name

Both your personal and professional e-mail messages sound warmer when you work the recipient's name into the last sentence. They know who it's from anyway. Reading "the sweetest sound in the English language" to them as the closing to your message creates a subliminal sense of respect and friendliness.

PART NINE

TEN LITTLE TRICKS

*to Make a Big Impression
on Your Cell (a.k.a. "Phone")*

How to Know When to E-Mail, When to Phone

Marshall McLuhan, the great Canadian educator, philosopher, scholar, and communications theorist, wrote, "The form of a message embeds itself in the message, creating a symbiotic relationship by which the medium influences how the message is perceived."

Happily, somebody shortened that to: "The medium is the message." Mr. McLuhan never heard of e-mail, but he would have said the same thing if he had.

He also would have predicted the problem that most of us still struggle with: "Should I phone him or e-mail him? Should I e-mail her or phone her?" In short, when is it more appropriate to phone, and when is it more appropriate to e-mail? Some things are better said, others are better read. Sometimes it's obvious, of course, but what about when it's not?

Let's say you are staying at a friend's house while she is working on an important project out of town. You are watering the plants, walking the dog, and feeding her ten goldfish. Sadly, one of them goes belly-up.

Oh dear, should I e-mail her? No, that's a little crass. Should I call her at the office? No, she's busy and might think I'm stupid to call her to the phone for one dumb little goldfish. After all, she does have nine others.

On the other hand, she might love those little ectotherms; when she gets back, she will be devastated. She'll scream at me, "Why didn't you tell me Parnell passed away?"

E-mail or phone? E-mail or phone? E-mail or phone?

Question Answered

Don't lose any sleep over it. There is a middle road. Figure out a time when you know the person is *not* going to be at the number you are calling, and leave a recorded message for him. Late at night is great for leaving voice mail at the office. Choose midday to leave a message at his home.

Be sure to preface your message with something like, "I know you're busy, so I didn't want to drag you to the phone. That's why I'm calling while you're out of the office." If it's true, you can add, "There is no need to call me back." That demonstrates extreme respect for his time.

Friends and lovers, you can use the same Little Trick. If, for personal reasons, you don't want to actually speak to your colleague or crush, leave an off-hours message. (Note that this is not recommended for breaking up with someone.) Now you can convey *precisely* the sentiment you wish.

Hearing smiles or frowns in your voice is more effective than reading smiley faces, which, as you know, professional types tell us not to use. (Except for Lisa Stracks, my wonderful copyeditor, who secretly told me she condones it for personal e-mail. But, shh, don't tell anyone I told you.) Phoning is more personal and is actually less time-consuming than reading an e-mail. And, if it is a delicate or legal matter, you are not leaving an e-mail trail.

 LITTLE Trick #82
Leave a Phone Message When You Know They're Out

When you don't want to drag someone to the phone but still prefer the personal touch, leave a phone message when she is not there. Between the lines, she'll know you are doing it out of respect for her busy schedule. Just in case, however, tell her, "Harley, I'm calling after hours because I didn't want to pull you to the phone just for this, but yada yada yada."

How to Boost Their Self-Esteem with Your Cell Phone

About a year ago, I received a call from man I thought was a big cat—but he swiftly shrunk to a little puss. Marty was the marketing director of an early dot-com company. Most of them became dot bombs by the turn of the century, but, as he told anyone who would listen, he "single-handedly saved the company." Marty had invited me to lunch to discuss the possibility of my training their customer service reps in telephone skills.

From his swagger into the restaurant, I sensed he was not the shy sensitive type. As soon as we sat down, he confirmed it. Like a Wild West cowboy slamming his gun on the saloon counter, Marty whipped out his cell phone and whacked it on the table next to his dessert spoon. Before I could even pick up the menu, his hand and phone were again in an embrace. After a barely audible "excuse me," he eagerly listened to his messages. I pretended that the menu mesmerized me until it finally dawned upon him he had a dining partner.

After the waiter took our order, we began chatting. Suddenly, I heard an infant crying, but where was it coming from? I turned around, but there were no babies in the restaurant.

Marty looked at me with a "hardy-har-har, fooled you" grin. As he picked up the howling phone, he proudly announced, "That's a recording of my kid crying. It drives the wife crazy." *She's not the only one. I am SO not going to work for you!* Being imprisoned in Marty's cell phone hell just wouldn't be worth it. His digital infant howled three more times during our lunch. Each time, he picked it up and looked lovingly into its little backlit face. He was calculating who was more important, the caller or me.

As we left the restaurant, I fantasized him as a baby crawling around the house in nothing but diapers with his cell phone attached by a big safety pin.

What About You?

How many times have you been chatting amicably with someone and suddenly your sentence is cut short by the sound of chimes, Beethoven's Fifth, Led Zeppelin, or salsa resonating from her pocket or purse? Like submitting to the spell of singing mermaids, she dives for her cell and stares at the screen for a second. Even if she deems you more important than the caller and puts it back in its resting place, the damage is done. She had no sensitivity to your feelings. No Emotional Prediction.

You probably think I am going to say, "Turn your cell phone off before meeting with someone." Sure, that's a good idea—but just average. Here is how to openly demonstrate your deference for someone.

One time, on a blind date, a Czech architect spun my heart like a top. Ivan Batucuda was good looking, but that was not the reason. He was well spoken, but that was not the reason. He seemed kind, but that was not the reason. Curious?

As soon as we sat down at the restaurant, without breaking eye contact or missing a word, Ivan reached in his pocket. I heard the power-down music of his cell under his voice. That sweet sound told me that, at that moment, I was more important than anyone who could possibly be calling him.

Did I hear someone say, "But that's manipulative. Why didn't he just turn off his cell phone before meeting you?"

My answer is this. "Is it manipulative when American soldiers salute a general? Is it manipulative when the Brits stand for the queen? Is it manipulative when Thai children kneel beside their elders on their New Year and wash their feet with lustral water?"

No, I say, they are demonstrating deference.

If the soldiers, citizens, or kids were saluting, standing, or spreading water all over the place ahead of time, generals, queens, and elders could not relish the respect they were expressing. And, if you turn your cell phone off ahead of time, your friend or colleague won't be able to witness and relish your esteem.

Little Trick #83
Let Them Hear You Turn It Off

Demonstrate your deference for someone by leaving your cell phone *on* until you sit down for the discussion, the dinner, or just "precious" time together. Then, at the very beginning of your rendezvous, reach for it. Without breaking eye contact, nonchalantly turn the potential interruption off. The lyrics to the power-down music are, "For these moments, you have priority over anyone in the world."

"Oops!" you ask, "What if I forgot to do this and it rings while I'm with the person?" Calmly proceed to the next maneuver.

For the Agile Only

Just like rolling a coin on your knuckles, the following move demands agility and practice. First, place your cell in its usual carrying position. Then rehearse reaching for it without looking and pressing the off key. But silencing it is not enough. Let them hear that sweet power-down song afterward.

This Little Trick is especially impressive if you execute it while speaking and you don't miss a syllable. Practice it a dozen times. You'll get the hang of it.

Here is another way to help people feel good about themselves—and therefore you!

How to Deal with a Caller When You Don't Know Who the Heck It Is

I'm sure it's happened to you. Your phone rings. You answer it. A cheery voice says, "Hi, this is Peter."

Peter? Peter who? I don't know any Peters.

Most people would ask precisely that, "Uh, Peter who?"

But because you have Emotional Prediction, you know Peter—whoever he is—would be devastated.

A rude Peter might respond, "You don't remember me? You know, from the golf course."

Mr. or Ms. Average would try to save the caller's face by saying, unconvincingly, "Peter, of course. I'm so sorry." But it's too late. Poor Peter feels forgotten, and you feel flustered. Not an auspicious start to a pleasant dialogue.

Let's do the numbers. Business researchers tell us we meet about a hundred people a year by name—social acquaintances, business contacts, and a few distant cousins who come out of the woodwork. About half of them will have the gall to think you should actually remember their names! Another half of that half could possibly contact you. And, for one reason or another, half of *that* half will.

You are now down to twelve and one-half people whose names you don't remember phoning you. Prepare yourself with the following face-saving (yours and theirs) rejoinder.

Ego-Saver When You Don't Know the Caller

Little Trick #84 not only saves the intrusive caller's ego, it conceals your memory lapse.

He says: "Hi, this is Peter."

With a big smile, say, "Hi . . . I know *two* Peters. Which one is this?" When he says you met at the golf club, sound like you are so pleased that it is *this* Peter, not that *other* one. If he just says his last name and pompously expects that to jog your memory, simply say, "From . . . ?" If he's the decent sort, he'll fill in the rest of your sentence. If he doesn't, you probably don't want to speak to the rude dude anyway.

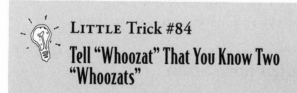

LITTLE Trick #84
Tell "Whoozat" That You Know Two "Whoozats"

When someone gives only her first name on the phone and you don't know who the heck she is, say, with as much congeniality as you can cough up, "Oh, I know two (fill in her name); which one is this?" There is a good chance she will give you her last name or the context in which you met.

How to Get Rid of "Talk Your Ear Off" People

Suppose a ruthless nonstop talker keeps blithering away on the phone, impervious to your entreaties that you need to go. If your conscience condones, execute the following Little Trick. There are three necessary tools: a sense of humor, one small purchase, and a touch of sadism.

Go to a toy store and ask for one of those plastic kiddie phones with an authentic-sounding ring. Bring it home, unwrap it, and place it right next to your real phone.

The Kiddie Phone Scam

Here's the tactic:

Step One: While Long-Winded Person is rambling on, press the ring button on the kiddie phone. Let it ring three times.

Step Two: Say to the nonstop talker, "Excuse me one second; my other line is ringing."

Step Three: Stop the ringing on the kiddie phone. Say to an imaginary Very Important Person, loud enough for the yapper to overhear, "No, no, hold on. I was just finishing up with this other call. I'll be right back."

Step Four: Return briefly to Windbag and tell him, "I'm so sorry, excuse me, I've been waiting for this important call that just came in."

Unless he is out for blood, he'll say "Good-bye."

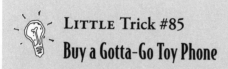

LITTLE Trick #85
Buy a Gotta-Go Toy Phone

Keep a realistic-sounding kiddie phone in reach of your real phone. If you make it ring and play your role, you can terminate your conversation with an agonizingly long talker in ten seconds or less.

I forgot the final step: give a fiendish sigh of relief after they hang up, and then kiss your kiddie phone.

The next Little Trick is a quick-as-a-cricket "click" that leaves people speechless with appreciation.

How to Please Them by Hanging Up on Them

Even the world's greatest scientist on time, Albert Einstein, would agree that time goes fast when you are having fun but seems interminable when you are not.

At this moment, you are listening on the phone to Ms. Loquacious. But you're in a frantic rush and tell her you have to go. She counters with, "I want to tell you just one more thing." Now every sentence she says seems ten times longer.

You've heard TV meteorologists say, "The temperature is forty, but the windchill factor makes it feel like thirty." Well Ms. L. talks only three minutes longer, but your annoyance factor makes it feel like thirty. A relationship can only take so many painful pricks like that.

When They Say "Gotta Go," *You* Go

One morning at about 11:30, I was speaking on the phone with a client, Michael Thomas, from Thomas Trucking in Illinois. Unfortunately, I had to finish up a project by noon and casually mentioned it to him. That would signal to most people that it was time to start winding down the conversation and talk only a minute or two longer. But not Michael. The next thing I heard was a friendly, "Of course, Leil, we'll talk again soon." *Click.*

I stared at the mouthpiece in amazement and admiration after he hung up. He had instantaneously understood my imperatives. I will always admire him for his Emotional Prediction and for giving me one of my most treasured telephone techniques: When someone says his time is tight, you have only ten seconds. Say one or two friendly sentences and hang up!

Another thanks to Lisa Stracks for tweaking this Little Trick. She and her friends, who are also moms, have a pact. When their kids start acting up, they've agreed, "Whoops, gotta go" is all they need. Smart!

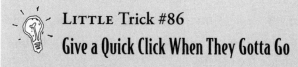

LITTLE Trick #86
Give a Quick Click When They Gotta Go

When someone tells you she is in a rush, do *not* keep her on the phone a second longer. As soon as she makes her urgency announcement, have mercy. Liberate her in one sentence or less. Caution: be friendly so she doesn't think you're hanging up on her.

At the end of a regular conversation, however, do just the opposite. When you and your phone partner are both hanging up, hold the receiver in midair for a few seconds before placing it in the cradle. In other words, be the last to hang up so a "click" is not the final sound he hears. You want the sound of your enthusiastic farewell, not a cold "click," to be his final impression.

How to Sound Cool Giving Your Phone Number

If the following Little Trick does not apply to you, please do not take it personally. Unfortunately, it did apply to me.

Whenever someone left me a voice mail message, I'd go scrounging through piles of paper and usually a hamburger wrapper on my desk to find something to write his number with. By the time I found a pencil, I had to listen to the message again to get the number.

Once when I was complaining to my office-mate, Doris, about what a pain in the gluteus maximus it was—and how I didn't want to inflict that pain on others—she gave me a business-savvy suggestion. She told me to leave my number at both the beginning and end of the message. "Doris, that's brilliant!" I cried. Feeling incredibly professional, that was my modus operandi for about a year.

But every time a caller did the same for me, I'd hear the number at the beginning and think, *"Uh-oh, it's now or never. Last chance. Do or die. I'd better write it down quickly, or I'll have to play the digital back-up game again."*

While scrounging for a writing instrument, I couldn't concentrate on the message and would have to play it again anyway. But I figured that was the best I could do until . . .

One day, I came back from lunch and checked my voice mail. It was my ex-husband Barry Farber, with whom I'm still close friends. His recording said, "Hi Leil, this is Barry. I'm at 765-4321. I'll give that number again at the end of the message. . . ."

Hallelujah! I had stumbled on the silver chalice of voice mail messages. I could concentrate on his message secure in the promise that he would repeat the number at the end.

My gratitude didn't persuade me to remarry him, but it did remind me of how brilliant he is.

LITTLE Trick #87
Give Them a Heads-Up That They'll Hear Your Number Again

Whenever leaving a voice mail message, give your number at the beginning of the message *and tell your messagee you will repeat it at the end.* He can then listen to your message at leisure while admiring your high EP level.

Speak Their "Numerical Language"

Here is a subtle tweak that most people will not even notice. But when big cats hear it, they assume you are a big cat, too.

People have different ways of giving and remembering numbers. Some people think in terms of individual numbers. They would say, "Seven six five, *four three two one.*" Others combine the numbers into small groups: "Seven six five, *forty-three, twenty-one.*"

Cover your bets to "speak their language." Give your phone number both ways. One form at the beginning, the other at the end.

Here is another auditory treat for your listeners. Do you remember the cyber-shrink's advice about putting the recipient's name last in your e-mail? The same obtains here. Think what a lovely little kiss it is to hear their own name at the end of your voice message. "Thanks, Ethan," or " I'm looking forward to hearing from you, Ethan." That closing has a nice ring to it.

At least to Ethan.

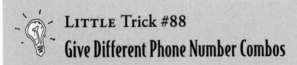

LITTLE Trick #88
Give Different Phone Number Combos

When you are giving your number twice on someone's voice mail, say it in a different grouping each time. Numberwise, you'll be speaking his language at least once.

And, as with e-mail, end your message with that "how sweet it is" word, his name.

How to Impress Them with Your Voice Mail Message

Several years ago, I got the rights back for a book I'd written for a publisher who had since gone out of business. I promptly proposed the book to another publisher. The next day, Arnold, one of the editors, called to say he liked it. Struggling to suppress a double back flip, screaming "YESSS!" I calmly asked him to tell me more.

He said the book needed a few rewrites, but he would submit it to the editorial board. Now in writers' sick fantasies, the editorial board is a tribunal of dukes, earls, and barons (called editors) who sit in the great hall of the publishing castle. Their massive marble table is piled high with manuscripts of wannabe writers. The king (the editor in chief) and his court convene for the sole purpose of sadistically rejecting the labors of us lowly serfs.

One week passed, no word. Two weeks passed, no word. So imagine my elation when I came home at six o'clock on a Friday and heard Arnold's voice on my answering machine: "I've got some good news for you, Leil. Call me back."

I wanted to sprout wings and fly. It was too late to call him back, so instead I picked up the phone and boasted to my two best friends. I told them, "We're going out to celebrate at El Costly Restaurant tonight, my treat." I would have a whopping dinner tab but, no matter, I'd make it up from the enormous advance the publisher was going to give me for the book.

Blue Monday

Needless to say, at 9:01 A.M. Monday I called Arnold for the details of the deadline, my advance, and so on.

"Hi Arnold, you left a message that you had some good news," I gasped breathlessly.

"Yes," he responded. "I'm leaving this publisher and moving to More Prestigious Publishing House."

Silence.

"Oh, well, gosh," I said. "That's wonderful. I mean, Congratulations. I'm uh, happy for you." And I meant it. I was happy for him. But not for me. As he droned on about his new opportunity, I tried to hear him over my self-centered thoughts:

Rats, that means I'm losing my shot at getting the book published because Arnold is the only one I know there. I'll be humiliated in front of my agent and friends. Worse, I'll get thrown back into that ocean of starving writers who are "between books."

My respect for Arnold didn't crash, but it lost a lot of altitude. Couldn't he predict my emotion—that I'd *assume* his message meant good news for me? Does that mean I like him any less? Not consciously. But the pain prick he gave me means he probably won't be the first editor I call when I have another book idea.

Before leaving any message for anyone, think hard. Has anything happened to him recently? What's on his mind? Whatever it is, address that first. *Then* give the part that concerns you. We often do this with e-mail but neglect it on the phone.

First, social calls: Your friend Erica has just returned from vacation. Don't just say, "Hi Erica. This is (your name). Give me a call." Leave this voice mail message instead: "Hi Erica. Welcome home. It's (your name), and I'm really looking forward to hearing about your trip. The leaves must have been beautiful this time of year in Connecticut. I hope you took some pictures. Call me back when you have some time to tell me about it."

For business calls, make it a bit shorter but still address their life first. Your colleague is in a sales conference this week? Say, "Hey Carl, hope your conference is coming along well and you're getting at least a little time to relax. I'm calling about . . ."

An Arnold with EP would have predicted my concerns and said something like this: "Hi Leil, I don't have an answer on your book yet. But call me back. I have some unrelated news." Those few sentences would have kept him flying high in my estimation. And I would have saved a couple of hundred bucks at El Costly Restaurant.

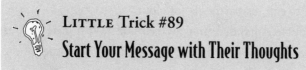

LITTLE Trick #89
Start Your Message with Their Thoughts

Before leaving a voice mail for someone, think it through. Is something on her mind? Is he awaiting an answer from you about something? Allude to that first. Then leave your message.

How to Make Your Phone Voice "Music to Their Ears"

One day a singer called me wanting to do some voice-over work through my small modeling agency that also provided performers for trade shows. I asked if he had a demo. He didn't, but the variety in his voice was phenomenal—everything from a loud laugh to serious direct inflections to passion when talking about his aspirations. I told him he could come later that day.

Zachary arrived about two thirty, and I gave him a short script to read. I was disappointed, however, because in person his voice didn't have that "magic quality" I'd heard on the phone.

As he was leaving, he said he'd left his cell phone at home and asked whether he could make a short local call. He had promised to call his partner before four.

Of course. I handed him my cell and told him to talk as long as he liked. He dialed as he walked to the far corner of the office so as not to disturb me.

At one point, I heard a loud laugh. Apparently, Zach was cracking up over something his partner had said. I looked up and saw he was holding the phone at almost arm's length. He then brought it back closer to his mouth as they discussed dinner plans for the evening. Then they must have been sharing something intimate because I could hardly hear him. However, I saw that he had practically pressed the phone against his lips. Moments later, laughter erupted again and, as before, he pulled the phone a couple of feet from his mouth.

When he hung up, he gave me an embarrassed smile and apologized, "I'm so sorry, Leil. I hope I wasn't too loud."

"Of course not," I told him. "It was interesting how you used the phone," I ventured.

"Yeah, people have commented on that. I guess I'm using it like the microphone when I'm singing." Hmm, that gave me an idea.

Could It Possibly Be?

"Zach," I said, "I hope I'm not holding you up, but could I ask you to read the script one more time into this?"

"Sure!" he said. I handed him a small tape recorder I had on my desk. Sadly, his reading wasn't much more impressive than the first time. As he was reading, however, he moved the recorder around from about two inches from his mouth to two feet. Sometimes he even varied the angle.

Afterward, we listened to the recording together. I was floored. It sounded fabulous!

Why? Because Zach's years of using a microphone for singing carried over into holding the phone at various angles and distances from his mouth. That was the reason for the fascinating variety I'd heard in our first phone conversation. I signed Zach up immediately for voice-over work.

I don't know where you are now, Zachary Thomas, but I hope you read this. I want to thank you for teaching me a wonderful Little Trick: vary the distances of the phone from your mouth.

Just as the microphone is part of a vocalist's magic, make different phone positions part of yours. It is not necessary for you to master the variety of distances that Zach used. Two are quite enough: close and far.

If the friend you are talking to on the phone makes a joke, you want to reward it with a big hearty laugh—but you don't want to blow his ears off. Hold the phone at almost arm's length and give his funny the big ha-ha it deserves. Do you want to tell your honey bun on the phone how much you love her? It sounds a lot sexier with your lips brushing the mouthpiece.

Your voice loses 30 percent of its energy on the telephone. In fact, many people speak in a relative monotone because they don't want to deafen their listeners with shouts, and they assume their whispers won't be heard.

Try it out by using a tape recorder first. You'll hear what I mean. Then add it to your bag of Little Tricks to captivate people.

LITTLE Trick #90
Move Your Cell Around Like a Microphone

Pretend your phone is a singer's microphone. Pull it away from your mouth when you are loud, and practically kiss it when you are whispering. Now there is no need to suppress your emotions. Be as effervescent or as sexy as you like by being a phone vocalist.

How the Phone Can Reveal Who the Boss Is in a Relationship

As a cooldown from our communication workout, we're going to stretch our mental muscles with a microtrick. This one is useful only to psychiatrists, people who sell big-ticket products, and those who have a perverse curiosity about the private lives of their friends.

I learned it from the Great Philosopher of Human Nature, Sal, the car salesman.

He called me recently and said, "Lil, I wanna tell you. The techniques you've been givin' me have made my sales go outta sight." I told him how much his overstated compliment meant to me.

"Yeah, yeah, thanks, Lil. But now I wanna give you one of *my* techniques that'll blow your socks off. Guaranteed."

"OK, Sal, I'm ready."

"Well, ya know, in my biz, I got to figure who is in charge, the man or the missus—who makes the buying decision.

"Now, here's the game. A couple is sitting at my desk, see? So I ask 'em a series of questions, any questions, like do they want cruise control, CD player—stuff like that. I direct my questions at both of them. Then I sit back and wait. I watch to see if the wife looks at the husband first or vice versa. If he looks at her for an answer, she's the boss. If she looks at him first, he makes the big decisions in the family."

"Hmm, that's interesting, Sal," I said.

"Wait. Wait, Lil. Here's the real clincher. While I'm sittin' there talkin' to them, I excuse myself. You know, they think I gotta go to the men's room or something. But I go into the back office and call their home phone. Any idea why I do that, Lil?"

"Uh, no, Sal. Obviously, they're not home."

"Right-oh. Usually their voice mail picks up. Now does that give you any hint on who's boss?"

"Uh, not really."

"I figured it wouldn't." He sounded as proud as a rat with a gold tooth when he told me. "I just listen to whose recorded voice I hear! The Top Dog is always the one who barks into the machine." He guffawed at his own joke. "Well, whadda ya think 'bout that one, Lil?"

I figured I owed him a compliment. "That's ingenious, Sal." But I wasn't sure he was right. I think he exaggerated when he said that in every couple there's a boss. I do agree, however, that one partner usually wields a bit more clout than the other in the big decisions.

My depraved curiosity persuaded me to conduct my own informal study. I listed all the married or living-together couples I knew. Then, mulling over what I knew about them, I calculated who might "call the shots" in important matters. I phoned each when I assumed Move Your Cell Around Like a Microphone they wouldn't be home.

Sure enough, most of the time, I'd hear the recorded voice of the partner I'd voted dominant. I had an 87 percent accuracy rate.

If their kids' voices were on the machine, that's another story.

Try it. But don't tell them what you've done. It's a fast way to lose friends.

What is all this leading to? Simply the fact that whose voice is on the home voice mail is more significant than you think. You take it from there.

Little Trick #91
Think Before Deciding Who Records Your Home Voice Mail

Now would I be so crass as to actually suggest you make sure it's your voice the next time you record the family voice mail? That would be unconscionable, right? Unless, of course, business colleagues might be calling you at home. In that case, make *sure* it's your voice.

My egalitarian suggestion, however, is to give up your land line and get two cell phones instead. Especially if your mate is going to read this book, too.

PART TEN

FIVE LITTLE TRICKS

to Deepen the Relationships
You Already Have

How to Win Their Hearts– a Year Later!

When a certain date rolls around on your calendar each year, do you get that silly faraway look on your face and indulge in happy reveries remembering a magnificent event in your life?

Was it when you graduated? Got your first job? Met your spouse? Gave up smoking? Adopted your beloved pet? Won the fifth-grade hula hoop championship? How sweet it is when your mind soars back. Your memories get big, and your pupils get small.

The special day I remember is when my first book came out. The publisher promised to send me ten copies. I waited anxiously by the mailbox the day I knew they would arrive.

When the postman came, I tore open the box and breathlessly showed him the table of contents. I tormented him talking about each chapter. Perhaps "Neither snow nor rain nor heat nor gloom of night could stay the courier from the swift completion of his appointed rounds," but I sure could. When the patient public servant finally broke away from my babbling, I bet he was contemplating writing a book himself . . . about the nut on his route.

On the next girls' night out, I chortled about my new work uniform—my pajamas. Ha ha ha. I crowed about my new work commute—from bed to the computer. Ha ha ha.

Why weren't they laughing?

A few days later, I dismounted my high horse and become human again. Life went back to normal. Although I did notice the postman avoiding me.

A Year Later

Cut to precisely 365 days later. I ambled to my mailbox but expected nothing special. However, I found a fancy handwritten envelope. Inside was a congratulations card. For what? From whom? When I read it, I was overcome with a severe case of the warm-and-fuzzies. Several of my friends who had suffered from my swelled head exactly one year previous to the date wrote, "Happy anniversary of your first publication date." I had to hold back the tears.

Of course, receiving a birthday or holiday card is lovely. However, it can't compare to the unexpected joy of receiving a note celebrating a happy personal event in your life. It is a law of human nature. The more original and unexpected a tribute is, the more people treasure it.

If you currently recall—or if you can dredge up—the precise date of something special in a friend's life last year, jot it down. Then commemorate it with a "personal event anniversary card" when that day rolls around this year. If your memory bank is currently empty, at least lay the groundwork for using Little Trick #92 next year. Start making note of happy events in friends' and colleagues' lives. It can even be something they told you about.

My friend Vicki Abraham said she fell in love with her future husband in a hot tub on Labor Day weekend. The following year, I sent her a "Happy Hot Tub Day" card on September first. She says she'll never forget it.

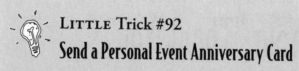

LITTLE Trick #92
Send a Personal Event Anniversary Card

Try to remember some accomplishment or special event in your friends' lives. Maybe the date he got a promotion. Or when your married friends met (divorced?). And, of course, don't forget the date their little bundle of joy was born. Or when the tot got her first tooth . . . the list goes on. And so does their appreciation of you when you send them a personal event anniversary card.

Another Reason I Like This Little Trick

I once had a tough boss, a textbook bully, who was bonkers about her cat. If she wasn't picking on me or barking orders, she was boasting about Bootsie. I wanted to go deaf every time she gave me the details of his diet, his hair balls, his birthday, and even his preferred kitty litter.

That was the year I had started remembering special events in people's lives. So I sent Bootsie a birthday card. I don't think I'm imagining it, but after that, things got a lot easier for me around the office.

How to Make Them Always Remember Your "Thank You"

When you were a toddler, your parents probably programmed you to say "thank you" when anyone gave you a present. They used to call it "bringing you up right." Now they call it "good parenting."

When someone gives you a gift, of course you must say "thank you." The words have become so common, though, that they sound like ambient noise. The bottom line is that the giver *expects* your thanks, and therefore it is nothing out of the ordinary. If you really want to thrill them with your gratitude, use the following Little Trick.

One year, I gave my friend Salina an inexpensive little music box. She sent me a thank-you note, which I appreciated—and, naturally, expected.

"Thank You" Is More Beautiful the Second Time Around

A few months later, I received an e-mail from her saying, "Leil, I can't tell you how much pleasure your music box continues to give the whole family. Instead of grumbling and diving back under the covers when I shout 'Time to get up!' the kids beg me to wake them to the sound of the beautiful music box you gave me. I wind it up and tiptoe into their room every morning. They wake up smiling, even before they've had their breakfast!"

Her message gave me more pleasure than the little music box could ever have given her. She made me feel like the Goddess of Gift Giving.

You've heard of a knee-jerk reaction? The doctor hammers your knee and your leg jerks. It's an involuntary response.

Saying "thank you" when someone gives you a gift is almost the same automatic response. But when you thank him again, weeks or months later—with all the reasons it continues to give you pleasure—you are giving him an even more valuable gift, the pride that he chose just the right present for you.

LITTLE Trick #93
Thank Them Again—Months Later

Whenever you thank someone for a gift, make a note to ponder the pleasure the present still gives you months later. Then thank her a second time, detailing how much you are enjoying it and why. She will find this second little thank-you more precious than the big first one.

And, incidentally, she will add you to her "extraordinary people" list.

Just as a simple "thank you" is so common that it loses a lot of its value, a *simple* compliment doesn't mean that much either. But a Little Trick #94 compliment packs a big wallop.

How to Give Them Compliments They'll Never Forget

It feels good when your supervisor, passing your desk, says, "Good job on finding that folder yesterday. Thanks."

But picture this. She comes to your desk in the morning, stops, smiles, looks you in the eyes, uses your name, and tells you, "I am really impressed you took it upon yourself to search for that missing folder yesterday." She continues, "You could have given up when it wasn't in the right drawer. But you stayed late and went through all the file cabinets. You didn't give up until you found it. Good job! Thank you so much."

That doesn't just feel good, it feels GREAT! Your smile lasts all day. Driving home, you are still purring. You tell your family about it at dinner. Suddenly you like your boss a whole lot more. Of course you'll go the extra mile for her again. No question about it.

Or picture this. You do a favor for a friend by taking her loudmouthed kid brother to the movies and Burger King afterward. As expected, he acts obnoxious the whole time. When you get back, your friend tells you, "Hey, thanks for taking Funny Face to the film for me."

You lie, "Sure, no problem."

That's the last time I take that little brat anywhere.

But what if your friend smiles and says, "Hey, thanks for taking Funny Face to the film for me. I'm sure watching a bunch of cartoon animals jump around isn't your idea of a fun afternoon. But he loved it! And when you took him to Burger King afterward, it was a fabulous surprise for him. He loves Triple Whoppers with cheese. He came home raving about it."

That's the least I can do for her. She really is a good friend.

Now you are a lot more apt to say "Sure!" the next time she asks you to baby-brother-sit.

It astounds me how rare this elongated kind of praise is. When criticizing someone, people stretch it out painfully long with all the gory details—until it really stings. But when people compliment, they usually spit it out in a sentence or two.

This Little Trick is easy, and the benefits are big. Simply expand your kind words by a few sentences. When they think you've finished, hit them with a few more. The melody and lyrics of your protracted praise make heavenly music for them.

A Riddle: Why Is This Technique like Foreplay?

You've probably guessed. The longer it lasts, the better it is.

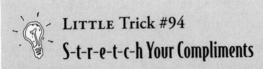

LITTLE Trick #94

S-t-r-e-t-c-h Your Compliments

Hearing praise is, in a sense, "making love" to someone. Don't make it "a quickie." Extend the verbal smooch as long as you can.

If you prefer, think of it this way: An actor relishes a round of enthusiastic applause. It is ecstasy when the audience won't stop clapping.

Would it be crass to mention at this point how much more the recipient will revere you for it?

How to Enhance Your Relationship with Your Partner

The man or woman we have chosen as a life partner is one of the—if not the single—most important relationships in your life. It's also the relationship most often abused.

When the romance is new, lovers look into each other's eyes and see ideal reflections of themselves. He sees a strong and capable man who has won his fair lady's heart. She gazes into his and sees a beautiful woman, inside and out. They feel good about themselves and their partner. They talk lovingly of each other to their parents, to their friends, and to anyone else who will listen. And they constantly praise their new partner.

Think about it. If either one spoke disparagingly of the other, the obvious question in everyone's mind would be, "Well, why the heck are you going to marry this person?"

As the years go by, the praise fades and denigration replaces it. How tragic it is that some insecure, insensitive people even complain about their partners to their friends. Don't they realize how it redounds to their own discredit? Between the lines, the listeners hear, "I have lousy taste in people. I am cruel, and I'm leading a life of quiet desperation living with that dimwit."

Shakespeare told us, "All the world loves a lover." He forgot to mention all the world hates a "disser."

When you express how splendid your partner or spouse is, everyone respects you. In essence, you are saying, "I chose the right person for me. I have my life together. I am happy and wise."

Make the Secret Not So Secret

In my relationship classes, I often ask couples, separately, to write which qualities and accomplishments they are most proud of and then which ones they admire most in their partner. Afterward, with their permission, the cards are paired up and read to the class. The results astound everyone. Seldom does anyone write that they love their mate for the same characteristics or triumphs their partner is most proud of!

What about you? Is your partner proud of being kind? Talented? Spiritual? Strong? Smart? Successful? Artistic? A wonderful parent?

Do you really know?

Ladies, suppose you are impressed that your man held down a job while he was in high school, owned a small business in his senior year, and was the Sudoku champion in his class. Gentlemen, you are thrilled that your lady was the high school homecoming queen, editor of the yearbook, and started a women's wrestling team.

Years later, at a gathering, the discussion turns to the good ol' high school days. Ladies, you boast your husband worked all through high school (i.e., he's hardworking) and even owned his own business (i.e., entrepreneurial). Gentlemen, you burst with pride as you tell the group your wife was the homecoming queen (i.e., beautiful) and the yearbook editor, too (i.e., smart).

Unbeknownst to your wife, however, you aren't that proud of your early business achievements. You want the group to know you were the clever Sudoku champion.

And when your husband told the group that you had been homecoming queen, you secretly thought, "The heck with all that shallow superficial stuff." You want them to know what an innovative and strong woman you were pioneering a female wrestling team.

As the wise philosopher Yogi Berra said, "One never know, do one?"

Listen to your partner carefully when talking with others. Read between the lines to determine which self-qualities please him or her. Which subjects does she like to talk about? Which would he like to show off his expertise on? Those are the ones to broadcast to gain respect and admiration for both of you. Not to mention the pride and passion it puts back into your relationship.

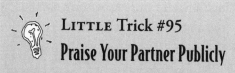

Little Trick #95
Praise Your Partner Publicly

Whenever you are talking with others, together or apart, allude to how exceptional your partner is—even how proud you are of him or her. You especially enhance the relationship if you tout not just the qualities and accomplishments *you* admire, but those that are the source of his or her self-esteem.

How to React When Your Partner Calls You the Wrong Name

Has your partner ever called you by somebody else's name? What was your reaction? Shock? Hurt? Anger? Suspicion? Sure, we chuckle when Grandpa gets the kids' names confused. It's a family joke that Aunt Nellie can't keep her nieces and nephews straight.

However, if you call your spouse or main squeeze by another person's name, look out! It can raise doubts, start fights, cause weeks of crabbiness, and even plant the seeds of separation.

But whoa! Stop. Let's analyze this. A person's name is no more than an arbitrary jumble of letters the hospital put on your birth certificate. Your high school positioned it under your photo in the yearbook. The government put it on your passport. Someday a stonecutter will carve it into your gravestone.

Naturally, friends and lovers remember your name—at normal times, that is. However, given a battle between their memory and strong emotion, the latter is going to win out. Especially when it concerns intense feelings like pain, illness, and anger. Ditto extreme joy, love, or sexual ecstasy.

Let's take sickness as an example. The average man unabashedly reverts to being a little boy when he gets sick. My ex-husband, Barry Farber, was no exception.

Chicken Soup Cures Everything

To my knowledge, there is no medical data supporting the curative effect of chicken soup for the flu. But Barry believed otherwise. At the onset of his symptoms, I was banished to the kitchen to prepare him a pot of it. While I was stirring the noodles on the stove, I heard him call from the bedroom, "Ullllllla, come here." I was livid because Ulla was the name of his first wife, a Swedish nurse.

The only reason I didn't throw a fit was because he already felt sufficiently wretched with the flu. I decided to wait until he recovered before making him more miserable.

An Insight That Could Help Save Your Relationship

After suffering the Ulla abuse, I stormed off to the grocery store. Fortunately, I happened to run into Sidney Gertz, a friend who is a well-respected psychologist. So I laid the entire Ulla story on him right there in the canned soup aisle.

He said, "Leil, names are attached to emotions. Barry's first wife was a nurse, right?"

"Well, yes."

"In his feverish state, I'm sure he remembered Ulla with fondness. She was a professional nurse who gave him excellent care when he was ill. Therefore, it was flattering when he called you by her name. It signifies that he thinks of you as a loving nurse."

"You've got to be kidding, Sidney! Are you telling me it was a compliment when he called me by her name?"

He nodded.

"Hmm," I mumbled, "well, Ulla did take good care of him when he was sick."

Your Partner by Any Other Name Is Sometimes Sweeter

"OK," I told Sidney. "But he better not try it when he's better!"

"Wrong again, Leil. It depends completely on what is going on at the moment. Haven't you ever called someone by the wrong name?"

"Yee-es . . ."

"In what context?" he asked.

I thought about it and realized Sidney was right. Sometimes Barry and I would argue. And, to this day, if someone infuriates me, in a moment of anger, I find myself calling him, "Barry!"

What About You?

Does your husband call you by the name of his deceased wife whom he loved? That is good. Does your wife call you by the name of her ex-husband whom she hated? That is not. Does your "faithful" partner shout out an unknown name at intimate moments? That's grounds for divorce.

Little Trick #96
Wrong Name, Right Sentiment

Someone calls you by the wrong name? Don't get upset. Get analytical. Consider the context. Ponder your partner's or friend's emotions connected with the name she called you.

To enhance your connection with that special someone, tell her you understand why she called you that. Then thank her for the transference of good feelings.

A Tip for Singles

Here is council if you are a single serial-dater. Give the person you are currently seeing a nickname: "Babe," "Honey," "Lovebug," "Lambchop." Then give the same nickname to your next partner. And the next. And the next. That way, you'll never goof up!

A Final Visit to the Laboratory

Do you remember the two gentlemen we met in the Introduction, the CEO and Joe, the floor cleaner? There was no noticeable difference between them—until they said their first words. The CEO recognized Joe's discomfort, then said, "Good job!" He also sensed that scientists need to feel their research is significant, and he expressed confidence in the professor's study. He instantly connected with both men and made them feel good about themselves.

Based on that small sample of his sensitivity to the floor cleaner and the professor, the CEO probably uses many of the Little Tricks we've learned: He offers praise to his employees when they deserve it and wins their loyalty by laughing with them. I'm sure he never talks about his wealth around those less fortunate or uses words too big for his employees.

The CEO has also prepared himself for corporate tiger attacks with strategies to look authoritative and to defend his actions from verbal assaults. Because he wants to provide a good life for his family and his employees as well as himself, he knows how to meet important people, get them to accept his invitations, start good networking conversations, change the subject when necessary, and escape incessant talkers. His e-mail messages connect with recipients. His telephone voice is persuasive. And, of course, he signs his letters in blue ink!

But what about poor Joe? From the small sample of his self-centered comment, "Glad I could help you out," he probably never thinks to make people feel good about themselves or to save them from embarrassment.

He has few friends because he never studied strategies to connect with people by starting good conversations and making people comfortable chatting with him. You probably wouldn't invite Joe to *your* party for fear he'd ask another of your guests, a doctor, to put down his martini to inspect a mole.

And, of course, poor Joe would have progressed further professionally if he hadn't forwarded jokes on company time or sent self-centered, insecure-sounding emails with thoughtless subject lines. He probably even blurted out phrases that made him sound as though he had no status at work.

Almost half a century ago, the Beatles wrote, "I get by with a little help from my friends." Times have changed, but that reality hasn't. Whatever you want in life, you need friends. Nobody gets to the top alone. As I wrote in the Introduction, "Unless you are auditioning to host the Academy Awards, your personality and looks are not the keys to becoming beloved and successful in life." So what is the key?

It is being able to *connect* with people. How? By consciously predicting people's emotions to whatever you say or do, then acting with sensitivity. These Little Tricks are a great start to get you practicing Emotional Prediction.

Some Real People You've Met in *How to Instantly Connect with Anyone*

There are a number of people I'd like to thank for demonstrating extraordinary EP and inspiring the 96 Little Tricks. With their permission, here are their real names:

Arturo Elias, the president of GM Canada, from Oshawa, Ontario, for his handshake that makes a powerful connection by touching the shakee's wrist vein;

Salina Fischer, from San Francisco, for sending me a *second* thank-you note saying why her kids love the music box;

Tova Svensson, the flight attendant from Orebro, Sweden, for the Little Trick of complimenting people behind their backs—loud enough for them to overhear;

Diana Parks, the speaker from Jackson, Mississippi, for advising me not to use strictly formal grammar when speaking to those with less education;

Cheryl Mostrom, the meeting planner from Phoenix, Arizona, for asking me loads of questions *just about my last few hours*, thus showing how it creates an instant connection and easy conversation;

Jonathan Rahm, the horse whisperer from Suffolk County, New York, for the incredible power of watching people's faces when they think no one is looking;

Roberto Magrini, the chef, and Foster Anderson, the Hewlett-Packard salesman, from Chicago, for mutual "horn-tooting"—making people eager to meet the other by speaking highly of each other ahead of time;

Giancarlo Parodi, my roommate Sandi's new boyfriend from Sanremo, Italy, for speaking exaggeratedly slowly to connect with people who were not as fluent in his language;

Camille Maziotti from Poughkeepsie, New York, for inspiring the schtick name trick by her big smiles when I call her "Dr. Camille";

Jan Storti, my new friend from Sarasota, Florida, for showing that being slower to join a conversation—but then being very participatory—is an impressive and likable quality;

Sidney Gertz, the psychotherapist from New York, for convincing me to consider the context when someone calls me by the wrong name;

Ivan Batucuda, the architect from the Czech Republic, for teaching me how to demonstrate deference by *not* turning a cell phone off ahead of time, but doing it audibly at the beginning of your conversation;

Michael Thomas, the trucking company president, for showing how impressive it is to hang up the phone immediately when people say their time is tight;

Barry Farber, the broadcaster from New York, for demonstrating a clever way to leave messages on voice mail;

Giorgio Accornero, the ship's captain from Genova, Italy, for using slightly squinting eyes to make people crave acceptance, then a slight smile to grant it;

Walter Correra, the CellularOne manager from Bermuda, for demonstrating the power of hearty laughter with professional or social subordinates; and

Robin Dawson, my friend from Evanston, Illinois, for teaching me how to avoid humiliation when I haven't a clue what people are talking about.

I'd also like to express my gratitude to a few other people who prefer that I use just their first name:

Gakuto, the Japanese businessman, for demonstrating respect by holding my business card in both hands;

Jimmi, the company president, for two prestige-enhancing Little Tricks: sitting in the highest seat or to the right of the big shot, and showing agreement with someone by nodding one's head up, not down;

Zachary, the singer, for showing how to make your telephone voice exciting by varying the distance of the receiver from your mouth;

Sandra, the new claims adjuster, for not immediately blurting out effusive apologies for her tardiness and showing a cool way to do it later;

My friends Ebony, Sammy, and Scott for party maneuvers like making an introduction pact with a friend; looking well connected by waving at imaginary friends; smiling at newcomers in the doorway; escaping incessant talkers; and showing me the advantages of arriving early at a gathering; and

My girlfriends Deborah, Vicki, and Patricia for sending me a "Happy Pub Date" card on the anniversary of my first book.

And thanks to a few strangers who inspired Little Tricks to save people from embarrassment:

Robert's mother on the bus, who cleverly covered my gaffe about her child's gender by instantly changing the subject;

My seatmate on the plane for answering me with different words the second time to save me from realizing I'd stupidly asked her the same question before;

And, of course, hundreds of males who have proven, beyond a reasonable doubt, that they do *not* like sitting with their backs to the door!

Connection: Your Best Investment

I'm sure you will succeed in whatever you seek in life. How do I know? Because, by reading this and similar books, you are investing your time and money in yourself and your relationships. It's the best investment you can ever make!

Please stay in touch. You can write to me through my website, lowndes.com. It may take a little time, but I promise to answer your message. You can also sign up for my free monthly "Little Trick" for big success in relationships. And, of course, I'd love to hear the Little Tricks you have used to win the business, the friendship, and the love you so richly deserve.

# Bibliography

Aronson, E., et al. "The Effect of a Pratfall on Increasing Interpersonal Attractiveness." *Psychonomic Science* 4 (1966): 227–28.

Birtchnell, John. *How Humans Relate: A New Interpersonal Theory.* Westport, CT: Praeger, 1966.

Carnegie, Dale. *How to Win Friends and Influence People.* New York: Pocket Books, 1936.

Cheek, J. M., and A. H. Buss. "Shyness and Sociability." *Journal of Personality and Social Psychology* 41 (1981): 330–39.

Cook, Mark. "Gaze and Mutual Gaze in Social Encounters." *American Scientist* 65 (1977): 328–33.

Curtis, Rebecca C., and Kim Miller. "Believing Another Likes or Dislikes You: Behaviors Making the Beliefs Come True." *Journal of Personality and Social Psychology* 51, no. 2 (1986): 284–90.

Dodd, D. K., and Markweise, B. J. "Survey Response Rate as a Function of Personalized Signature on Cover Letter. *Journal of Social Psychology.* 127 (1987): 97–98

Dressel, F., and Paul Atchley. "Conversation Limits Attention: The Impact of Conversation Complexity." *Journal of Vision* 5, no. 8 (1973): 398.

Dunn, Elizabeth W. "Misunderstanding the Affective Consequences of Everyday Social Interactions: The Hidden Benefits of Putting One's Best Face Forward." *Journal of Personality and Social Psychology* 92, no. 6 (June 2007): 990–1005.

Gladwell, Malcolm. *Blink: The Power of Thinking Without Thinking.* New York: Little Brown and Company, 2005.

Goleman, Daniel. *Emotional Intelligence.* New York: Bantam Books, 1995.

Harrison, Albert A. "Exposure and Popularity." *Journal of Personality* 37, no. 3 (1969): 359–77.

Hayakawa, S. I. *Language in Thought and Action.* New York: Harcourt Brace Jovanovich, 1941.

Keller, Paul W. "The Personal Enjoyment of Conversation." Paper presented at the Annual Meeting of the Central States Speech Association, Minneapolis, 1973.

Lavrakas, J. "Female Preferences for Male Physiques." *Journal of Research in Personality* 9, 324–34

Leary, M. R., and R. F. Baumeister. "The Nature and Function of Self-Esteem, Sociometer Theory." In *Advances in Experimental Social Psychology*, vol. 32, edited by M. P. Zanna, 1–62. New York: Academic Press, 2000.

Lewis, David. *The Secret Language of Success.* New York: Carroll & Graf Publishers Inc., 1989.

Lieberman, David J. *Instant Analysis.* New York: St. Martin's Griffin, 1997.

Lowndes, Leil. *How to Be a People Magnet.* New York: McGraw-Hill, 2001.

———. *How to Make Anyone Fall in Love with You.* New York: McGraw-Hill, 1996.

———. *How to Talk to Anyone.* New York: Contemporary Books, 2003.

———. *Undercover Sex Signals.* New York: Kensington Books, 2007.

Martin, Peter A. "Psychoanalytic Aspects of That Type of Communication Termed 'Small Talk.'" *Journal of the American Psychoanalytic Association* XII (1964): 392–400.

McKenzie-McHarg, Kirstie. "Effect on Survey Response Rate of Hand-Written Versus Printed Signature on a Covering Letter Randomized Controlled Trial." Oxford University Research Archive, 2005.

McNeil, Daniel. *Face: A Natural History.* New York: Little Brown and Company, 2000.

Morris, Desmond. *Manwatching: A Field Guide to Human Behavior.* New York: Harry N. Abrams, 1977.

———. *The Naked Ape.* New York: Dell, 1967.

Neuberg, S. L., and S. T. Fiske. "Motivational Influences on Impression Formation: Outcome Dependency, Accuracy-Driven Attention, and Individuating Processes." *Journal of Personality and Social Psychology* 53 (1987): 431–44.

Nierenberg, Gerard L., and Henry H. Calero. *Metatalk.* New York: Trident Press, 1985.

Oetting, E. R. "Examination Anxiety: Prediction, Physiological Response and Relation to Scholastic Performance." *Journal of Personality and Social Psychology* 3 (1966): 224–27.

Sannito, Thomas, and Peter J. McGovern. *Courtroom Psychology for Trial Lawyers.* New York: John Wiley & Sons, Inc., 1985.

Schimel, Jeff, et al. "Being Accepted for Who We Are: Evidence That Social Validation of the Intrinsic Self Reduces General Defensiveness." *Journal of Personality and Social Psychology* 80, no. 1 (2001): 35–52.

Stevens, L. E., and S. T. Fiske. "Motivation and Cognition in Social Life: A Social Survival Perspective." *Social Cognition* 13 (1995): 189–214.

Tannen, Deborah. *Talking from 9 to 5.* New York: Avon Books, 1994.

Wojciszke, B., W. Baryla, and A. Mikiewicz. "Two Dimensions of Interpersonal Attitudes: Liking Is Based on Self-Interest, Respect Is Based on Status." Unpublished manuscript, Polish Academy of Science, 2003.

Wojciszke, B., R. Bazinska, and M. Jaworski. "On the Dominance of Moral Categories in Impression Formation." *Personality and Social Psychology Bulletin* 24 (1998): 1251–63.

Zweigenhaft, Richard L. "The Empirical Study of Signature Size." *Social Behavior and Personality: An International Journal* 5, no. 1 (1977): 177–86.